OLD-FASHIONED
Christmas Gifts
TO MAKE FOR FAMILY & FRIENDS

OLD-FASHIONED
Christmas Gifts
TO MAKE FOR FAMILY & FRIENDS

Diana Mansour

House Editor: Dorothea Hall
Editor: Diana Mansour
Art Editor: Caroline Dewing
Stylist: Kay McGlone
Production: Craig Chubb

Copyright © Marshall Cavendish Limited 1988

The edition specially produced for The Leisure Circle Limited
by Marshall Cavendish Books Limited

Printed and bound in Hong Kong by
Dai Nippon, New Territories

Contents

Introduction

Thou day of happy sound and mirth
That long wi' childish memory stays
How blest around the cottage hearth
I met thee in my boyish days . . .

from *The Shepherd's Calendar,* 1827,
by John Clare

Christmas is traditionally a time for laughter, for reconciling old differences, for parties and presents, and above all a time for sheer enjoyment of life, an oasis of exuberance in the desert of winter. Nowadays, unfortunately, it can also be a time of harassment, of spending more money than we can afford on things that we don't really want, of senseless competition and increasingly frayed tempers as the day itself draws near.

However much we may wish to preserve the Christmas message of peace and goodwill to all men, there is a tendency to become trapped in a commercialized parody of the old Christmas traditions – pagan and Christian alike – and to spend endlessly, not only on presents, but on all the other accessories, such as wreaths, tree decorations, cards, wrapping paper, Christmas napkins and table mats, and stockings. Yet Christmas is still there to be enjoyed, and most of us have an inner picture of our own ideal Christmas, influenced by happy childhood memories and pictures from Victorian story books, in which the decorations and presents remain but the commercial element is removed.

This book offers an escape route away from the over-commercialized twentieth-century Christmas and shows how easy, and how much more enjoyable, it is to make your own decorations and small gifts, cards and wrapping paper, stockings and table mats. With a little care and thought, the end results can be every bit as attractive and just as beautifully co-ordinated as the goods on offer in the shops, but you will feel a far greater satisfaction when your guests compliment you on your lovely decorations and you are able to reply that you made them yourself.

However commercialized Christmas becomes, children will still enjoy the day itself, but it is the run-up to the festive season that can easily become so joyless. In the last century, each household would be a hive of activity during the days before Christmas as everyone, children just as much as grown-ups, made little trinkets and boxes to hang from the tree, prepared small gifts for relatives and special friends, gathered greenery and wove it into wreaths and garlands, and generally participated to the full in the fun and excitement of preparing for the event. All of this enjoyment, and the resulting sense of achievement, is lost if all the goods are bought ready-made.

The different chapters of this book contain a treasury of Christmas designs. A few, such as the knitted stockings, require specific skills, but the majority could be made by a complete beginner to the crafts involved, and many could be used as family projects, with children joining in the fun. Some items, such as the embroidered card, would take a little time to produce and are likely to be reserved for favoured friends and relatives, but others can be made so quickly that you will wonder why you ever bothered to buy them in previous years. So try out some of the designs shown here, and experience some of the pleasures of an old-fashioned Christmas.

CHAPTER 1

The holly and the ivy

For so many of us, the transformation brought about by Christmas decorations is an essential part of the festive scene, and everything connected with it, from gathering bunches of evergreens to the spraying and painting and binding, and then the final moment when you stand back to admire the effect, is unforgettable fun. Traditionally the gathering of the greenery and its hanging takes place just before Christmas, but a little forward planning can make an enormous difference to the finished effect. Think of Christmas before pruning any evergreen trees and shrubs in your garden; gather and store nuts and pine cones in the late autumn, and keep cuttings of lavender, rosemary and thyme to be included in decorations – their perfume will be released by the warm air to give your home a delightfully refreshing Christmas atmosphere. In addition to door and table decorations, the following chapter offers evergreen swags and posies including a child's candy wreath, plus a hanging bough made from dried grasses, and fun paper streamers in the shape of shooting stars.

Materials

25cm polystyrene ring filled with
  absorbent foam (available from florists)
Short lengths of holly, variegated holly,
  cypress, yew and pine
White everlastings *(Helichrysum)*
Dried poppy seed heads
Cow-parsley seed heads
Pine cones
Holly berries – artificial, from florists
Gold spray
Red poster paint
2m of 2.5cm-wide ribbon
Stub wire (available from florists)

Door wreath

These days many people buy their
door wreaths ready-made, but in fact
they are so easy to make and so
rewarding that it is a shame not to give
yourself the pleasure and satisfaction
of making your own. Provided you
carefully select the most perfect sprigs
of greenery and decide in advance
whether you intend to produce a
wreath highlighted with gold or silver,
or one that displays the traditional but
always effective contrast of bright red
and deep green, there is no reason
why your wreath should not look
every bit as good as any that a florist
might produce. Bear in mind the
colour of your own front door: it may
be that a different colour scheme from
those suggested above would
integrate better with the colours of
your house. The wreath described
here is only an example, illustrating
the basic construction of a wreath, and
you will almost certainly find that you
are adding your own individual
touches.

Preparation

Leave the ring to soak in water, so that
the foam absorbs as much as possible,
while you prepare the seed heads and
pine cones.

  The seeds and flowers included in
this wreath are only suggestions:
others, such as the silvery, rounded
seed pods of honesty, may be more
readily available to you and would be
equally suitable.

  If you are using cow-parsley seeds,
spray them with gold and leave them
on newspaper to dry. Also spray some
of your pine cones with gold. Paint
others with red poster paint.

  If the seed heads are to be used in
small clusters, cut 20cm lengths of
stub wire to bind them together. If
they are to be used individually you
will still find it easier to cut the stems
and bind them with lengths of wire.
The pine cones should be wired in a
similar way: cut a 20cm length of wire

and wrap the centre of the wire
around the lowest layer of pine petals;
bring the ends together under the
cone and twist them together.

  Fix a length of wire through and
round the ring and shape it into a
small circle at the back to make a
hanger.

Making the wreath

It is best to work with the wreath in
place on the door. If you do not have a
door knocker at a suitable height, you
will have to hang the wreath on a
small nail.

  Start by inserting short lengths of
cypress and yew around the outer

edge of the circle until the outer frame is well covered. Next, insert small pine sprigs around the inner circle, making sure that you keep the centre well shaped.

Next, position the cones, pushing the lengths of stub wire firmly into the foam. Use gold cones at the base, then place red ones around the circle and put clusters of berries at the top.

The next stage is to fill in all the remaining areas with a well-balanced mixture of variegated and green holly.

Step back frequently and take a look to make sure that the effect is balanced. When the wreath is well covered, add the seed heads, everlastings, and artificial berries, if needed. Finish by cutting the ribbon into two equal lengths and making a large double bow to pin at the base of the circle.

From time to time over the holiday, take the wreath down and lay it on the ground so that you can replenish the foam with water.

Evergreen posy

A bunch of evergreens to hang on a door or to decorate a wall or an archway is one of the simplest – and prettiest – of seasonal designs, and because it is so very simple and uncluttered it can have a sophistication that more complicated arrangements sometimes lack. These little posies are so quick to make that you can easily substitute fresh greenery if the first sprigs start to look tired before the holiday is over.

Preparation

If you are using spray paint, lightly spray the twigs and lay them out on newspaper. When they have dried, turn them over and spray the other side of each twig.

Attach a length of stub wire to each nut and cone (see page 12), ready to bind them to the stems. Prepare the baubles in the same way, threading a length of wire through the loop at the back of each one.

Making the posy

When all the stems have been prepared, lay them on your table or work surface. Place the longest and widest ones in position first, in the form of a shallow fan, and arrange the other stems over them. Take care to alternate the colours and textures of the leaves to avoid a flat, heavy look.

When you are happy with the arrangement, bind the stems firmly together with wire. If you have too many bare stems gathered at one end you can cover these with a few shorter lengths of foliage.

Twist the wired nuts and cones securely to the stems, then do the same with the baubles, first inserting short lengths of wire through the loops of each bauble and twisting firmly to hold.

If the decoration is to hang indoors, or in a porch, it may not be necessary to wire the nuts. Push a piece of blue tacky clay or a sticky fixing tab on one side and it can then be pressed firmly to a twig (see above).

Take a short length of ribbon and tie it around the stems in a bow, with short tails. Repeat this with the second length of ribbon, this time leaving long tails of ribbon to trail down the bunch. Trim the ends neatly into inverted arrows.

Attach a length of wire to the back of the posy and use this to hang it from the door.

Materials

A selection of evergreens such as pine (you can use off-cuts from the Christmas tree), ivy trails, laurel, bay, cypress and holly, and some well shaped twigs such as apple (these should be green wood, not dried twigs, which might snap)
Cones, nuts and small Christmas tree baubles to decorate the stems
Fuse wire to bind the stems
Stub wire to attach the nuts and cones
Gold or silver spray paint (optional)
1.5m of 3cm-wide ribbon

Materials
25cm polystyrene ring filled with
    absorbent foam (available from florists –
    this makes two horseshoes)
Short lengths of evergreens, such as yew,
    cypress, pine, holly and ivy
A few pine cones and glossy chestnuts
30 florist's holly berries (if the holly
    has no real berries)
1m of 4cm-wide florist's ribbon
1.2m of narrow ribbon or gold cord (if
    wreath is to hang with ends upwards)
Stub wire (available from florists)

Horseshoe wreath

Here's a traditional welcome with a difference – a lucky horseshoe of bright and shiny evergreens to hang on the door. For added luck, make sure that it contains plenty of holly, traditionally supposed to be hateful to witches. Another tradition was that if the first holly brought indoors at Christmas time was prickly, then the man would have the mastery for the coming year; conversely, if it was smooth then the woman would rule: but perhaps Christmas is not the time to be thinking of disputes, even the battle of the sexes. Depending on the positioning of your door furniture, the horseshoe can either hang as shown in the picture, or you can fix lengths of ribbon or gold cord to the sides and suspend it from these, so that the wreath hangs with the two ends pointing upwards, in the traditional manner.

Making the wreath

Start by cutting the polystyrene ring in half: it will cut easily if you use a sharp bread knife. Use one half and set the other to one side to make a second horseshoe or a table decoration (it

can be used to make a pretty half-circular frame of greenery around a candle on a side table).

Soak the half circle of foam that is to be used for the horseshoe. Start inserting the evergreen sprigs, working from the centre out to one end and then out to the other. To make sure that you have a balanced effect, it is a help if you first divide the greenery into two evenly mixed bunches. Alternate smooth and shiny foliage and spiky stems as you work. Press longer stems into the two cut edges so that the design tapers away neatly.

When you have finished inserting the greenery, wire the pine cones and nuts (see page 12) and press these in randomly but evenly around the wreath. Lastly, twist artificial holly berries around the stems, if needed.

Form the florist's ribbon into a bow and thread a length of stub wire through the back of the loop. Press the wire into the foam at the centre of the wreath. If the horseshoe is to hang with its ends upwards – traditionally believed to hold in good luck – cut the ribbon into three equal lengths and form three bows with shorter tails – one for the centre, one positioned about a third of the way up one side and one placed closer to the top at the other side.

If the wreath is to hang pointing downwards, take a length of stub wire and wind it around the wreath at the central point, making sure that the wire is hidden by foliage and the bow. At the back of the wreath, twist the wires together and then form them into a loop for hanging, see page 12.

If the wreath is to hang with the ends pointing upwards, take two lengths of stub wire and wind one around each end of the wreath, making small loops at the back, as described above. Cut the narrow ribbon or gold cord into two lengths and thread one end of each through a loop and tie, then tie the other ends in a bow at the hanging point.

Materials

Thick sash cord, cut to length as required (see below)
Approximately 500g of sphagnum moss (available from florists)
Fine wire, such as fuse wire, for binding
Short lengths of evergreens – holly, ivy or cypress
Christmas tree baubles
Florist's holly berries – approximately 40
Pine cones
Stub wire (available from florists) sufficient for pine cones, baubles, ribbon bows and bunches of berries
4m of 4cm-wide tartan ribbon for bows
Fine masonry nails

Evergreen ribbon

If the main focal point of your room is a fireplace, then you have the perfect setting for a truly traditional swag of evergreens and pine cones. The evergreen ribbon featured here does not, of course, have to be set over a fireplace: it could be arranged above a doorway or an arch, around picture frames or even around a window. If it could be swathed around a mirror then you would have the double benefit of the reflection.

Hanging

Start by deciding exactly where the ribbon is to hang and how. Fine masonry nails, of the type used to hang pictures, are very unobtrusive and should not leave any visible mark, but if you are worried about damaging your wall you may be able to avoid inserting new nails if you can use existing picture hooks.

   Any nails should be hammered in at a slightly sloping angle for added strength.

   When you have decided where the swag is to hang, loop a length of string in that position and then measure it to find how long your sash cord should be. Remember that the sprigs of evergreen at either end will increase the length to some extent. Cut the cord to the required length.

Making the ribbon

Take handfuls of the moss and wrap it around the cord, then bind it over and over with thin wire until you have made a moss-padded sausage about 4cm in diameter. Measure the padded cord and mark the centre point.

   Cut even lengths of evergreens and group them into small mixed bunches – cypress, holly and ivy, for example – to ensure that you achieve an even distribution of the different types and colours along the length of the cord.

   The next stage is to start binding the sprigs to the cord. If it is to lie flat against the wall, then you will want to

make sure that the sprigs lie to the front and sides, so lay the cord on a flat surface and use this as a guide while you work. If the finished ribbon is to be draped over a mirror, bear in mind that the back will also be visible to some extent.

Start at the centre of the rope and work first to one end. Place a bunch of evergreens on the rope, with the stems to the centre, and bind it firmly in place, passing over and over the stems with the fine wire. Arrange each following bunch so that the stems are concealed by the tips of the previous one.

Reverse the rope and start from the centre again, working out to the other end. Make a small cluster of leaves and bind them to the centre of the swag to conceal the overlapping stems.

Finishing and mounting

Using stub wire, bind the holly berries together in small bunches, leaving a sufficient length of wire to attach each bunch to the swag. Wire the pine cones (see page 12) and thread stub wire through the loop at the back of each bauble.

Spacing them in an attractive but random pattern, push the wires holding the berries, cones and baubles into the moss.

Cut a 1.2m length of the ribbon and tie it into a bow for the centre of the swag. Pass a wire through the loop at the back and push it into the moss. Cut the remaining ribbon into six equal lengths and form each into a bow, then wire them to the swag in the same way.

To hang the swag, wind lengths of wire round it at the hanging points, concealing the wire under the sprigs, and tie the wires firmly to the nails or picture hooks. Adjust the outer edges of the foliage to give a feathered look.

Evergreen candy wreath

Pretty and eye-catching, and with a tasty promise of things to come, this candy wreath would make a lovely gift, whatever the age of the recipient. Lacy posies of shiny wrapped sweets adorn a ring of evergreen foliage interspersed with crosses bound with red satin ribbon.

The result is a charming wreath which can be hung on a wall or door or even placed at the centre of the table, ready to be demolished at the end of the meal. If family and guests are content to feast with their eyes instead of their mouths, it can be saved as a last treat before the decorations come down on twelfth night.

The foliage
Choose thick, bushy sprigs of foliage.

If necessary they can always be trimmed. The ring will look much more attractive if more than one type of foliage is used. The most suitable trees to choose would be coniferous firs, using a dark variety for the background and overlaying this with sprigs taken from a tree or bush of a brighter green and with a slightly different growth habit. If you wish to relieve the green, you could perhaps add a few sprigs from a golden cypress. If you do not have access to a garden and must buy your foliage, trim the stems and immerse the sprigs in water for a few hours before making up the ring.

Making the ring
Using the thicker wire, make two rings, one 20cm in diameter and one 25cm, each formed from three circles of wire and held together with

Materials
The following materials are sufficient to make a 25cm-diameter ring.

Ring
Ready-made florist's wire ring, 23cm to 25cm in diameter
or two rolls of green-coated garden wire – one of medium thickness and one thinner and more pliable
Wire-cutting pliers
4m of black or dark green wide bias binding
Black or dark green tissue paper – a sufficient length to wrap around the ring in a loose spiral
Black or dark green sewing thread
Selection of evergreen foliage sprigs, each 10cm to 15cm long
3m of 1cm-wide red satin ribbon

Posies
30 shiny wrapped sweets – 15 each in red and green (if you want to use unwrapped chocolate truffles or after-dinner mints so that the wreath can form a table centrepiece for a dinner party, then use small quantities of foil paper in different colours)
1.50m of 4cm-wide red satin ribbon to hang the ring
1.50m of pre-gathered broderie anglaise or lace edging
1.5m of green-coated garden wire for tying

adhesive tape at four evenly spaced points.

Place the smaller ring inside the larger one and, using the thinner wire, lace them together by double-twisting the wire around each ring alternately, working progressively around until the two rings are firmly fixed together. Twist any sharp ends so that they point inwards.

Take a sheet of tissue paper and loosely roll it up along its length, then very loosely twist the paper cylinder into a spiral. Lay it around the front of the wire circle to give bulk to the top (visible) side. You may find that you need to use more than one sheet of tissue to cover the entire circle.

Open out the bias binding and press it flat. Use the tape to bind the tissue paper to the rings, passing the tape in and out of the rings and working around in a spiral. Take care not to crush the paper, and overlap the previous round of binding by approximately a third of its width at each turn. In this way pockets will be formed into which the sprigs of foliage can be inserted.

Take the darker foliage first and strip off the lower leaves to expose about 4cm of stem. Working always in the same direction, insert the stems under the overlapping bands of binding. Build up the ring in this manner until it looks sufficiently dense and bushy, finishing off with lighter-coloured foliage. Use smaller sprigs to fill in any thin-looking areas.

When the ring looks sufficiently well-covered take the reel of thread and bind round the foliage, placing the thread under the surface greenery to keep it out of sight. The ring should now appear attractively solid and the foliage well secured. Any pieces that protrude beyond the others can be lightly pruned.

The posies
The six posies shown on this ring have been made using clusters of five sweets, but more or fewer could be

used according to the size and type of sweet being used.

Take dark sewing thread and tie it first around the end of one sweet then bind it firmly to the next. Holding the ends very firmly in the fingers of one hand, continue to tie in further sweets, winding the thread tightly around each one several times and in and out of the other sweets in random directions until they are all very firmly bound together at one end only. Make six groups of sweets in this manner.

Cut the pre-gathered broderie anglaise into six 25cm lengths and sew small running stitches along the gathered edges. Draw each one up to measure 10cm and fasten with several small stitches. Sew the raw edges together thus forming a gathered circle of lace.

Take each cluster of sweets and twist a short length of wire around its base. Place inside the broderie anglaise ring and fasten the whole posy very firmly to the fir wreath by winding the wire round the ring.

Finish off by cutting the narrow red ribbon into two equal lengths of 1.50m. Secure the ends on the underside and, working in opposite

directions, wind both lengths around the ring so that they form a cross between each posy. Use the wider ribbon to tie a bow at the top of the wreath.

Straw wreath

Based on the ancient country craft of making corn dollies, straw figures to symbolize the forces of fertility and ward away evil, here is a charmingly rural wreath festooned with loving hearts and Christmas stars to bring you luck now and in the coming year.

You can buy the various elements used in the making of this unusual hanging wreath from a craft shop, but it would be infinitely more pleasant to gather them for yourself from the countryside on a warm afternoon in the late autumn and store them ready for the festive season. If you cannot find pine cones of the appropriate size you could wind trails of ivy around the ring, to alternate with the ribbon, or attach attractive dried seed heads taken from your garden.

Making the ring

First cut the birch twigs. The finished ring shown here measures approximately 35cm in diameter and 3.5cm thick, when bound. The twigs must be fresh and pliable (twigs found on the ground may be too brittle) and the leaves must be stripped off. If you do not have silver birches in your area, use other canes or twigs (sweet chestnut is very pliable, and it may help if you soak the twigs in water overnight).

Form the twigs into a ring and bind them firmly together with garden twine. It is important to make sure that the ring is completely symmetrical.

Take the grass or raffia and carefully bind it round the twigs until they are completely covered.

Take the red ribbon and wind it around the ring in a spiral, leaving

Materials

Silver birch twigs (or similarly pliable twigs)
Dried long, wild grass stalks (alternatively use straw-coloured raffia)
20 small pine cones
Straw or wheat stalks – approximately 100 and 20cm long
7m of 2.5cm-wide red ribbon
Fine card
Red tissue paper
Gold paper stars (obtainable in sheets from stationers)
Garden twine
Dressmaker's pins
Cream and red sewing thread
All-purpose glue
Scissors
Scalpel or craft knife
Tracing paper

Trace pattern for hearts

Large hearts

Small hearts

about 2.5cm of grass showing through between each turn of the ribbon. When you have worked around the ring, cut the ribbon and secure the ends with dressmaker's pins, stuck into the ring.

Take the pine cones and attach these to the top of the ring with glue, spacing them evenly around the circle.

The hearts

The hearts are all made in the same way. Trace over the heart outlines and either cut out the tracing paper shapes and use them as templates or use carbon paper to mark out five large hearts and three smaller ones on the card. Cut these out.

Draw around the inside of each heart shape, 3mm from the outer edge, and very carefully cut along this line to leave a narrow heart-shaped outline in card.

Cover the outline lightly with glue and lay it down over red tissue paper.

Make sure that the paper is absolutely flat – if necessary first press it with a warm iron to remove any wrinkles. Position about six paper stars on the larger hearts, spacing them evenly but at random over the tissue paper, on the side with the card edging. You may

prefer to use self-adhesive stars, or use a tiny amount of glue for each star.

Cut out the shapes, then once more put glue around the card edge and, turning the hearts over, place them on the tissue paper again so that both sides are now covered and the stars are enclosed. Cut around the outline of each heart once more.

Thread a needle with red sewing thread and make a neat knot at the end. Draw the needle through the centre point at the top of a large heart so that it is held by the knot. Push the other end through the ring, so that the heart can hang down from the ring by a thread approximately 6cm long. Suspend three more large hearts from the ring in the same way, spacing them an equal distance apart.

In the same way, link the remaining four hearts together: attach the centre top of one small heart to the lower tip of the remaining large heart, leaving a 2cm length of thread between them; attach the centre top of the large heart to the lower tip of another small heart, with a 3cm length of thread between them; attach the remaining heart to the chain with the same spacing. Set this chain of hearts to one side.

Straw stars

Take the lengths of straw and flatten them with the blunt side of your craft knife, working from both sides of the straw until each piece is completely flat. To avoid damaging the work surface, cover it with newspaper or card.

When you have several flattened straws, you can start making the stars. They are all made following the same principle but you can vary the stars by using different lengths and thicknesses of straw.

For the first type of star, take four lengths of straw approximately 8mm wide and 9cm long, and four thin straws approximately 4mm wide and the same length as the others. Holding them steadily between thumb and forefinger, arrange two thin straws to cross each other at right angles, then add the other two to cross each other, lying in between the spaces left by the first two. Add the four thick straws to complete the star shape so that there are 16 spokes radiating outwards from the centre, with thick and thin straws alternating.

Take about 50cm of cream sewing thread and, leaving an end approximately 15cm in length, wrap the thread around one of the straws and tie a knot. Make the tie as close to the centre of the star as possible and make sure that you do not crush the straw. Work around the centre, carefully taking the thread alternately

over and under successive straws, gently moving your finger and thumb out of the way as you work, but keeping a firm hold on the star. When you have worked all the way round and back to the beginning, wrap the thread around the first straw again and then repeat the process, this time working anti-clockwise and taking the thread under the straws that it passed over the first time, and vice versa.

Tie a knot and trim the thread so that both ends are 15cm long. Trim the straws so that they are all the same length, then shape the points with a pair of sharp scissors. You can alternate points with inverted points, or clip them into arrow shapes, as shown.

Make several variations, working to the same basic method. Some of the stars shown here, for instance, are made by crossing 12 thin straws and cutting half of the spokes back to within 2cm of the centre, so that long and short spokes alternate around the star.

Make a total of eight stars of varying forms. Thread the ends through a needle and attach the stars to the ring so that there are two evenly spaced stars between each heart.

Finishing

From the remaining ribbon cut two 75cm lengths and attach them with dressmaker's pins inserted into the centre of the ring, so that the four ends are evenly spaced and are secured at the points from which the four hearts will hang.

Take the remaining length of ribbon and tie it in a large bow at the point at which the two ribbons cross over. Leave one long end from which to hang the circle.

Using a needle and red thread, as before, run a length of thread through the centre top of the first heart in the chain and take the other end through the central bow, so that the hearts will be suspended from the centre of the ring.

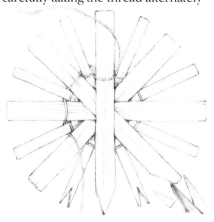

Shooting stars

Large gold or silver stars, linked with multicoloured, star-scattered trails, make a dramatic room decoration, far more elegant and effective than the majority of purchased paper decorations. The stars are three-dimensional, made from carefully assembled pieces of gold card. The number required and the length of trail to allow between stars will depend on the size and dimensions of your room, including the height of the ceiling, so before starting to make this decoration, experiment by holding loops of paper streamer or even string against your walls to help you to get the proportions right. Once you have decided on the distance between the stars, these positions can be lightly marked using either a soft pencil or dressmaker's pins. Similarly, the choice of strands to make up the trails can be varied to suit your room scheme and to match your other Christmas decorations. In fact, last year's paper streamers and tinsel may be given a new lease of life if used in this way.

Materials

42cm x 29.5cm of light-weight gold
   or silver card for each star
Selection of rolls of crêpe paper and
   coloured foil for the streamers
Light-weight gold or silver card for
   small stars (optional)
Tracing paper and pencil
Craft knife or scalpel
Metal ruler
Clear adhesive

Small star

For best results, use templates to cut
out these stars from gold and silver
card. Using a soft pencil and ruler, first
trace off two stars, as given, and
transfer the outlines to the card,
turning the tracings over before going
over the outlines with a ruler and
pencil. Cut out the templates using the
scalpel and ruler. Make as many stars
as required to decorate the trails.

Large star

The shape provided forms one point
of a five-pointed star, so trace the
shape and then transfer this to the
back of the card. Cut it out carefully,
using the craft knife or scalpel and
ruler, then use this shape as a
template to mark out as many points
as you require for the number of stars
to be made.

   On each point, the dashed lines
represent folds; the dotted line marks
the edge of tab 3, which is left flat out
and lies under the adjoining point.
Carefully run along the fold lines,
pressing with the blunt side of a knife
or with a knitting needle, and then
fold them. Glue tab 1 under edge 1 to
make a pointed shape with one raised
side (the front) and one flat side (the
back). Make four more points, then
assemble them together by gluing tab
2 under the sloping edge 2 of the
adjacent point and tab 3 under flat
edge 3 until you have formed a five-
pointed star.

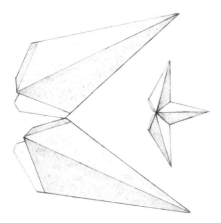

Trace pattern for small stars

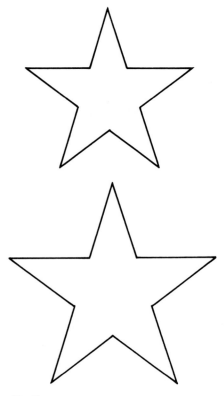

Trails

When you have as many stars as you
require, make the looped trails,
attaching them at the points which will
be covered by the stars. Use a variety
of strands of crêpe paper and foil,
experimenting until you have a
satisfactory effect. Place thicker strands
at the back and lay thinner strands on
top. Pin or tape the strands in position
around the room then place the
smaller, flat gold stars in between the
trails, scattering them at random to
give the effect of sparks of light from
shooting stars.

Finishing

Finally, place the three–dimensional
gold stars in position, with the flat
centre back of each star covering the
point where the looped trails are
attached to the wall. Use double-sided
tape, tacky clay or sticky tabs to hold
the stars in position.

Trace pattern for large star point

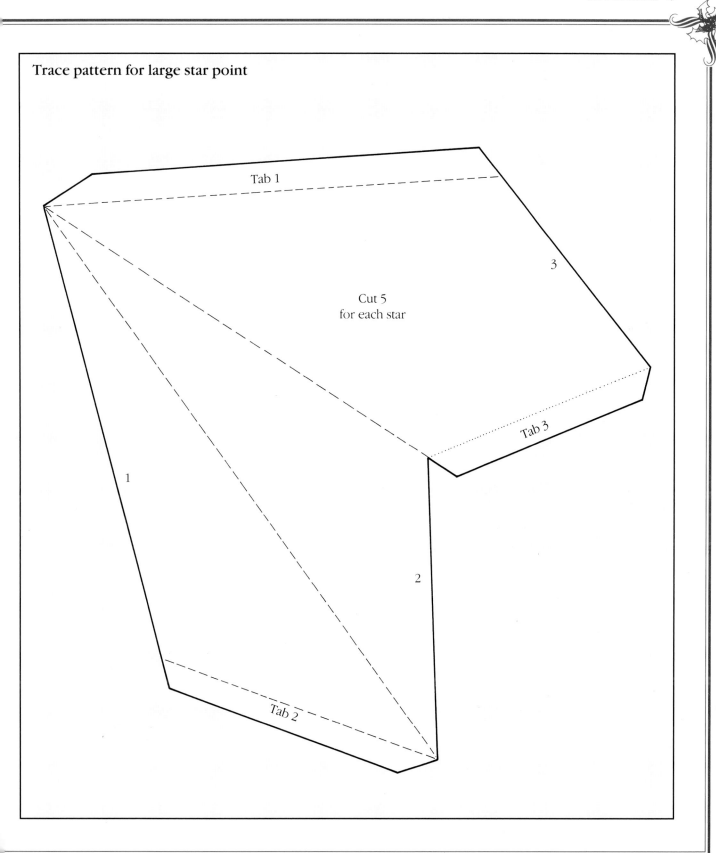

Tab 1

3

Cut 5
for each star

1

2

Tab 3

Tab 2

CHAPTER 2

Christmas tree, oh Christmas tree

Decorating the Christmas tree is an important part of that gradual build-up of excitement that children find so exhilarating at Christmas – by the time you stand back to admire your efforts the suspense will have become almost unbearable! And how much more pleasurable the finished effect will be if you have made some or all of the decorations yourselves, as people used to do in Victorian times. The decorations shown here include two alternative tree skirts, to conceal the base of the tree, wooden outline figures, little wreaths made from baker's clay, patchwork stars, paper snowflakes and baskets, padded angels and doves.

Materials

4mm birch plywood offcuts
Fine sandpaper
Satin finish varnish
Tracing paper
Pencils and pen
Fine artist's brush
Inks (see below)
Poster paints (see below)
Adhesive tape
Paper tissues
Gold thread

Father Christmas
Red ink
White, pink, blue and black poster
    paints

Angel
Yellow ink
White, pink, blue, black and gold
    poster paints

Star
Yellow ink

Snowman
White, black, green, red and
    orange poster paints

Heart
Red ink

Apple
Red, green and brown inks

Christmas tree
Green, red and brown inks

Candle
Green, red and yellow inks
White and black poster paints

Tools
Fretsaw (or electric jigsaw)
Drill with small bit
Carpentry clamp

Wooden tree hangings

Easily made from plywood, these
small shapes, brightly coloured with
poster paints, take very little time to
make and no advanced carpentry
skills. Use them as shown here, to
decorate a tree, or for other Christmas
decorations: you could hang
snowmen, angels or Father
Christmases at the ends of a chain of
cards, for instance, or you could try
your hand at making a mobile using
lengths of silver or green-coated
garden wire for the cross-pieces.

Father Christmas

Copy the pattern onto tracing paper
with a pencil. On the reverse side of
the tracing paper, draw over the lines
with a soft pencil. Place the tracing on
the wood, with the soft pencil lines
facing down, and using a harder
pencil trace over the lines, transferring
the design to the wood.

Drill a small hole at the top of the
hat, just below the bobble, to take the
thread.

Secure the wood to a solid surface,
using the clamp (if you are using a
good table, put card between the
gripping ends of the clamp and the
table, to protect the surface). Carefully
cut around the outline with the
fretsaw, taking care not to split the
wood at the edges of the shape.
Sandpaper around the edges, the front
and the back.

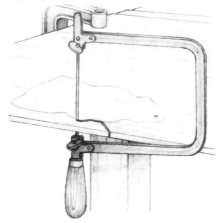

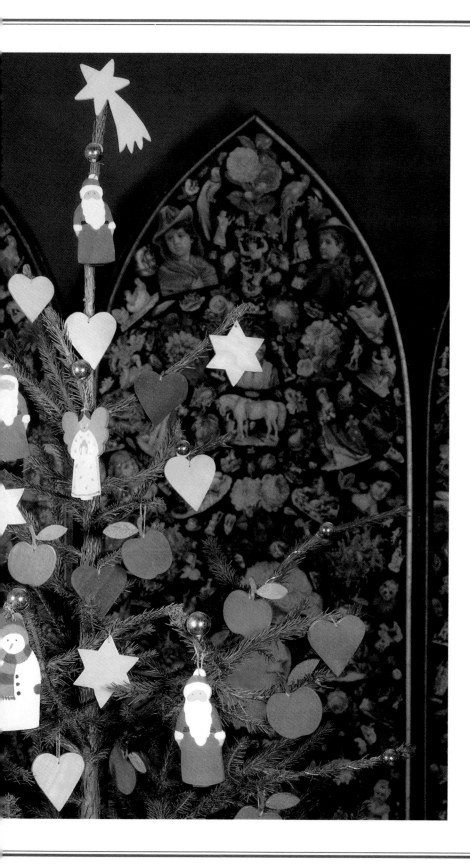

Using the fine brush and red ink, paint in all the red areas on the front of the design. Take great care where the red ends and another colour begins to make sure that the red does not bleed along the grain of the wood.

You can help to reduce this problem by dabbing away excess ink with a paper tissue each time you have made a brush stroke. Ink around the edges of the shape, to fit in with the line of the costume, then leave the shape until the ink has dried thoroughly. Turn the shape over and, still using the red ink, paint the red areas on the back of the figure.

Mix white paint to a fairly thick but still paintable consistency and apply it carefully to the front and edges, where appropriate. As with the red ink, leave the paint to dry before turning the shape over and painting the white areas on the back.

Repeat the process with the black paint for the belt and boots, the pink paint for the cheeks, and the blue for the eyes.

When the paint is completely dry, paint the front and edges with the varnish and leave it to dry. Turn the shape over and repeat the process on the back. Give the decoration two complete coats of varnish.

Cut a 20cm length of gold thread, push one end through the hole and make a tie.

Angel
Trace and cut out the shape as for Father Christmas. Paint the yellow ink on the front and edges of the wings and, when dry, on the back. As when applying the red ink to Father Christmas, use a paper tissue to dab any excess ink away as you paint.

Next apply poster paints in the following order: white for the dress, black for the hair, pink for the cheeks, blue for the eyes and gold for the halo and the dress details. Always paint the front and sides first and leave this layer to dry before turning the shape over and painting the back.

Varnish and hang the angel as described for Father Christmas.

Star
Make in the same way as described for Father Christmas, using yellow ink for the front, edges and back.

Snowman
Trace and cut out as described for Father Christmas. Apply the paints in the following order: white, red, green, black and then orange. In each case, paint the front and edges first, then turn the piece over when the paint has dried and paint the back, before moving to the next colour.

Finish with two coats of varnish and thread with a gold tie, as for the other shapes.

Heart
Make in the same way as the other shapes, using red ink for colouring.

Apple
Make in the same way as the other shapes. Apply the paints in the following order: red, green and then brown. In each case, paint the front and edges first, then turn the piece over when the paint has dried and paint the back.

Trace patterns for wooden tree hangings

Angel 1

Angel 2

Star

Heart

Father Christmas

Apple

Snowman

Materials
A selection of bronze, gold and silver papers is generally used, or you might decide to make all your baskets from either a mixed variety of colours or just two colours, to match your chosen Christmas décor – gold and blue, for instance, or silver and red. For one basket you will need:
22cm x 11cm of paper in each of two
   colours
Tracing paper
Ruler, pencil and felt-tipped pen
Paper scissors or scalpel
Paper glue
Medium-weight card

Heart baskets

These pretty little paper baskets are so easy to make that they are quite simply child's play – a traditional pre-Christmas pastime for generations of children from Victorian times onwards. The technique is so simple and effective that it takes very little time to produce several baskets, made from a variety of coloured papers. Although they are made only from paper, each basket is sturdy enough to hold a few sweets or chocolates or small gifts for a children's party.

Paper weaving
If you plan to make a whole collection of baskets for your tree, you will need to make a template from thin card. Start by tracing the basket pattern given below. Glue the tracing to the card and carefully cut out using a ruler and scalpel to cut all straight edges, and taking care when cutting in between the inner strips. (See making a template on page 43).

Place the template on coloured paper with the short edge to a fold, as instructed, and cut out. So as not to waste paper, place each shape next to each other, butting the straight edges.

The next stage may sound complicated, but in fact it is very easy to do if you have the pieces of paper ready to use. Take the two main pieces and hold them at right angles to each other, with the folded ends adjacent. Take the first folded strip of colour 1 and push it through the first folded strip of colour 2. Open the first strip of colour 1 a little to make a loop, and pass the second strip of colour 2 through the loop. Close the loop of colour 1 and push it through the loop of the third strip of colour 2, then push the last strip of colour 2 through the loop of colour 1.

One strip of the first colour has now been woven into the second piece of paper. Repeat the process with the three remaining strips, alternating the process to create a woven effect. When the last strip is woven in, the basket will hold itself in a secure shape when opened.

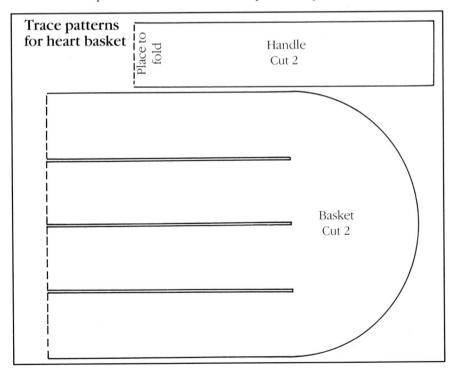

Trace patterns for heart basket

Place to fold

Handle
Cut 2

Basket
Cut 2

Take the two strips for the handle and glue them with wrong sides together to make a two-coloured handle strip, then glue the handle to the basket, with one end at the centre of each side of the heart, and placing the ends about 2cm inside the basket.

Hang the basket on your tree with a few sweets or a small gift inside.

You can vary the weaving pattern by taking some strips over two strips instead of one strip of the second colour – the best way to discover what will look attractive is to experiment.

Snowflakes

Light, delicate snowflakes hanging from a tree or festooned around a room make delightfully pretty decorations, a charming seasonal contrast to festive swags of greenery highlighted with gold and with red ribbons. The outlines seen here are copied from real snowflake crystals, which appear in an infinite variety. The snowflakes themselves are designed in such a way that they can be as simple or as complicated as required: single crystal shapes to hang against a wall, or three-dimensional flakes formed from two, or for maximum effect three, interlocking circles. The flakes seen here are made from plain white card, but you could equally well use foil (two sheets glued together would give double-sided foil with extra strength) or coloured card.

Preparation

There are six spokes on a snowflake crystal, and the three-dimensional snowflakes are made up from quarter crystals, each with one and a half spokes, glued to central circles of card. The single snowflake can either be formed from four quarters glued to a central card circle, or you can cut it out in one piece, in which case you will not need a card circle.

To transfer the outline to the thin card or cartridge paper you can use one of several methods: if the paper is sufficiently transparent it may be possible simply to place it over the outline and trace through; or failing this, you could trace the outline and make a card template (see page 43), or you could trace the outline and then transfer it to card. The tracing can be used repeatedly if you turn it over after each use and trace down from the other side. Any pencil smudges on the card can easily be removed after you have cut out the shape.

The single snowflakes are four separate or repeated quarters; the double flake is made from eight separate quarters, joined with two card circles (these only require slit A in order to interlock), and the elaborate snowflake is made up from 12 pattern quarters plus three card circles, one of each type shown. Although the pattern quarters needed to make up the double and elaborate snowflakes can all be of the same type you may prefer to vary the effect, by using four of one type and four of another to make up the double snowflake, for example.

If you take care when cutting out the outlines it is possible to cut out two layers at once, even from thin card, so you only need to mark out half the total number of outlines which you will require.

Cut out the snowflake pattern quarters and interlocking circles, using a craft knife or scalpel. First cut out the shapes roughly, cutting about 1cm outside the marked outer line. Cut the second, unmarked layer of card approximately 5mm larger all around than the marked layer and tape both to a spare piece of hardboard or similar small cutting surface which you can turn as you work.

Simple snowflake

Cut out a whole snowflake pattern or cut four quarters and glue these to a central circle. Gently erase any

Materials

Thin card or cartridge paper for the crystal-shaped outlines – the quantity will depend on the number and form of flakes required

Medium card for the central, interlocking circles

Tracing paper and pencil

Craft knife or scalpel

Clear adhesive

Transparent thread, for hanging

Sewing needle

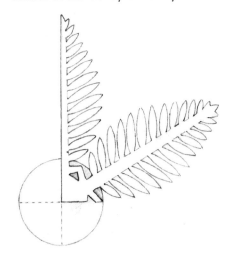

Trace patterns for snowflake quarters

Trace patterns for central circles

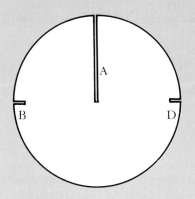

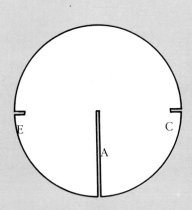

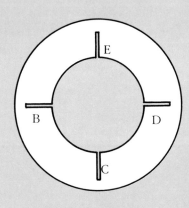

remaining pencil lines, then using the needle and thread make a hanger through the end of one of the crystal spokes.

Double snowflake
Take two card circles, each with slot A cut out, and fit them together through the slot into a spherical shape. Glue four snowflake quarters to each circle. Hang the snowflake as already described.

Elaborate snowflake
Cut three card circles, one with slots A, B and D, one with A, C and E, and one hollow circle with B, C, D and E. Interlock the first two through slot A, then carefully slip the third circle over the resulting spherical shape until it locks into position through the side slots.

Take twelve pattern quarters of the type given for the elaborate snowflake and position four around each card circle. Hang the snowflake as already described.

Materials

Medium thick card – approximately
 10cm x 20cm
Tracing paper
Spray glue
Scalpel or craft knife
Metal ruler
Writing paper or thin card
Small quantities of at least six
 dress-weight cotton fabrics
Small quantity of loose wadding
Matching sewing threads

Templates for stars

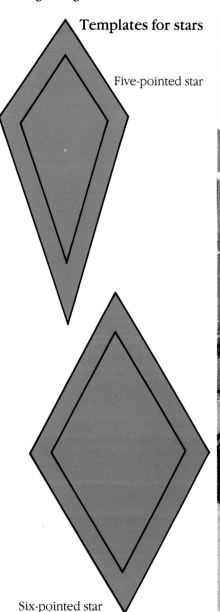

Five-pointed star

Six-pointed star

Stars, stars, stars

Give your Christmas tree a sweetly
traditional look by festooning it with
these dainty patchwork stars instead of
commercially produced plastic
baubles. Here are decorations which
are easy to make at odd moments, and
in fact because they are sewn by hand
you can even carry the work around
with you.

The five- and six-pointed stars are
made by joining diamonds together
using the English backing paper
method, which gives a very precise
finish – ideal for these neat little
decorations which will twinkle on
your tree year after year. You can use
small odds and ends from your scrap

bag, but it would be better to choose
small lengths (the minimum
quantities that you can buy) of
coordinating Christmas fabrics. Make
sure that all the fabrics are the same
quality and weight; ideally, dress-
weight pure cotton.

Make as many stars as you need for
your tree, plus a few extra ones to tuck
into your Christmas wreath and other
decorations, to carry the theme
through.

Five-pointed star

The five-pointed star is made with the
two more sharply pointed templates,
with the sharp points facing
outwards. Start by making two
templates. The smaller template will

be used to cut the backing papers; the larger template is used for the fabric shapes and therefore includes the seam allowances.

Trace over the two diamond shapes given, then cut them out roughly, leaving a margin of about 1cm around each shape. Using spray glue, stick the tracing paper shapes to the card, then carefully cut out the templates along the marked lines, leaning the scalpel against the metal ruler.

Making the stars
Each star is made from a total of ten diamonds – five for the front and five for the back.

Using the smaller template, mark as many diamonds as you will need for the required number of stars on the writing paper and cut them out. Using the larger template, mark and cut out an equal number of fabric patches, making sure that you distribute the patches evenly between the different fabrics.

To prepare the patches, centre a backing paper on the wrong side of a fabric patch and hold them together with a pin. Fold the seam allowances over the backing paper one by one and tack. Fold the seams in neatly at the wide angles, but allow the excess seam allowances to lie flat at the sharp points, so that they protrude beyond the backing papers.

Place two diamonds right sides together and oversew along one edge, taking approximately eight stitches to the centimetre and pulling the thread very tight. Do not stitch beyond the point of the backing paper. Join

another pair, then stitch the two pairs together. Add one more diamond to complete the star shape.

Make sure that the protruding tails all follow in the same direction so that they interlock neatly at the centre of the star, each tail lying over the tail of the preceding diamond.

When you have made two star shapes, pin them right sides together and oversew along the edges, folding and trimming as necessary to make neat points. Leave a small gap unsewn and turn the star to the right side through this gap, after first taking out the tacking and removing the backing papers by pulling them gently loose from the stitches.

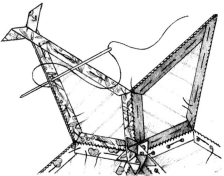

Gently ease out the points, using a knitting needle or a blunt pencil and push a little wadding into the star. Make sure that it is evenly distributed, right up to the points, and do not overfill. Close the opening with small, neat stitches.

To attach a loop for hanging, simply thread a needle with matching sewing thread or fine metallic thread and insert it through one of the points, about 5mm from the tip. Cut the thread to length and knot the ends together.

Six-pointed star
The six-pointed stars are made in exactly the same way as the others, but using the two remaining diamond templates. Make each star shape by joining three pairs of patches, and then joining the pairs into a six-pointed star.

Materials

For each bird
Tracing paper
Medium-weight cardboard
Spray glue
20cm of 90cm-wide polyester satin
Loose polyester wadding
1m of 3mm-diameter pearl trim
Two flower sequins
Two diamanté sequins
Fabric glue
Matching sewing thread
White bird
50cm of 3mm-wide white-and-silver
    ribbon
60cm of 1cm-wide pre-gathered lace
Blue bird
3m of 3mm-wide white ribbon
40cm of 3mm-wide blue ribbon
Peach bird
Six lace motifs
60cm of gold (picot) trim
50cm of gold cord
50cm of 3mm-wide gold ribbon
2 gold beads

Flight of fantasy

Doves of peace in white, peach or blue satin make highly appropriate but unusual Christmas decorations. Make a complete set to hang from a large tree, or just a single bird to decorate a Christmas wreath. The different trims added here are only suggestions – this is a chance to delve into your scrap basket for odds and ends of trimmings that were too pretty to discard. The finished doves measure approximately 13cm deep and 20cm from tip to tail, but if this is too large for your purposes make your templates smaller, adjusting the cutting and stitching lines, as required.

White bird

Trace the diagrams for the wing and body on tracing paper, glue the paper to medium weight card with spray glue and cut around the outlines to make templates.

Using the templates to transfer the outlines on the fabric, cut out one pair of bodies and two pairs of wings. Make sure that the grainlines of the fabric will all run in the same direction on the finished birds.

Place the two body pieces with right sides together and stitch around the outline, taking a 6mm seam and leaving an opening for turning, as

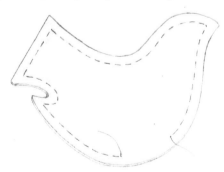

indicated. Sew the two pairs of wings together in the same manner, again leaving openings for turning. Cut notches from the seam allowances on outward curves and clip almost to the stitching line on inward curves then

turn the pieces right side out. Fill the pieces with wadding and slipstitch the openings together.

The eyes and trims, as well as the wings, are all attached with fabric glue. This must be done very carefully, so that no glue ends up in the wrong place. If any should get on your hands or the work surface, clean it away before continuing. Use a toothpick or a blunt-ended tapestry needle to apply the glue in fine lines.

Glue lace to the back of each wing, overlapping neatly at the wing tips. Apply pearl trim to the outer edge of each wing, so that it is backed by the lace. Again, start and finish at the wing tips. Glue pearl trim around the body, covering the seamline. Apply a flower sequin at each eye position, then add a diamanté sequin to the centre.

Glue the wings in position on the body. Cut a 26cm length of narrow white-and-silver ribbon, form it into a loop to make a hanger and glue the ends in position, as indicated on the diagram.

Take the remaining length of ribbon around the neck and form it into an unknotted bow. Glue it in position to complete the bird.

Blue and peach bird

The blue and peach birds are made in the same way as the white bird but with different trims. For the blue bird, glue strips of white ribbon to the wings before applying the pearl trim and tie a single bow around the neck. For the tails to the bow, cut two 40cm lengths each of blue and white ribbon, fold in half and glue in place. (You may prefer to hold these together with a few small stitches rather than glue.)

For the peach bird, attach gold picot braid to the wings in place of the lace trim of the white bird, and gold cord in place of the pearl trim. Glue lace motifs in position as shown in the photograph. Use gold ribbon for a neck tie and a hanging loop.

Trace pattern for bird

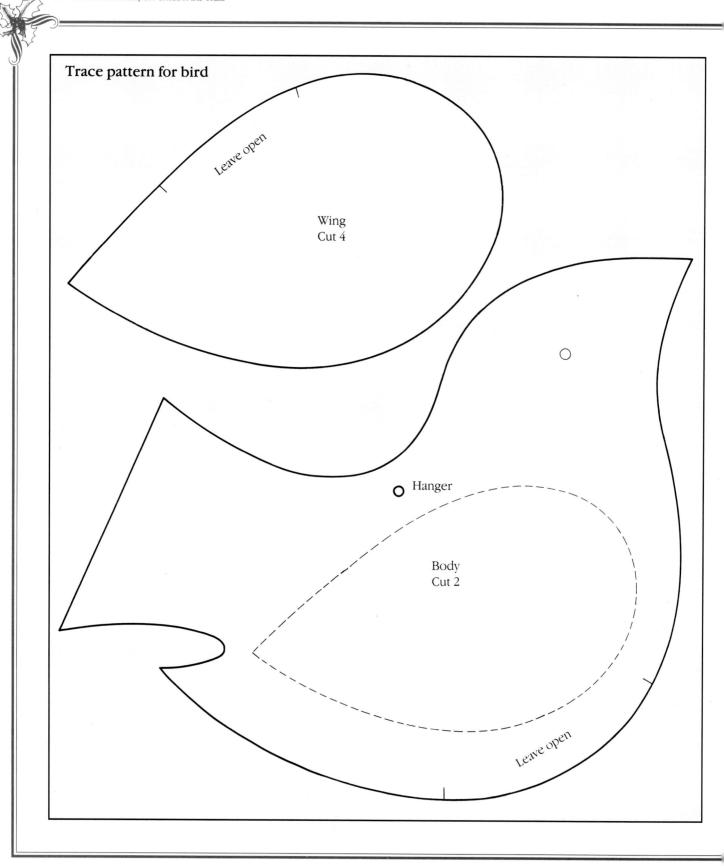

Leave open

Wing
Cut 4

Hanger

Body
Cut 2

Leave open

Calico angels

Make a little band of calico angels with round, smiling faces to hang from your tree and add a touch of beautifully home-produced cheerfulness. Each angel carries a different instrument or accessory, ingeniously made from such unlikely beginnings as a golf tee, and each is decorated with delicate hand embroidery and gold trimmings. The angels are not difficult to make, though the embroidery takes a little time, and you and your family can all have fun thinking up further home-made musical instruments for the band.

Each angel
Making the head
Using the permanent pen, draw a face on the large macramé bead (the drilled hole must run from top to bottom of the finished head). If you do not feel very confident of the result, draw the face in very lightly with pencil first so that you can rub or wipe off any mistakes. Otherwise, the black marker will adequately cover correct preliminary pencil marks.

Tease out the wire strands of the pot cleaner and cut away about a third. Glue the cleaner to the bead so that it frames the face.

The embroidery
Mark an oblong on the calico measuring 18.5cm x 10cm, using the ruler and pencil. Decide which embroidery pattern you wish to use – each dot on the pattern represents one French knot – and again using the pencil, lightly indicate the pattern on the calico. Place the lowest points 1cm up from one long marked edge (this becomes the bottom edge) and make all markings on the wrong side of the fabric.

Using perlé thread, embroider the pattern of your choice, making French knots (see below) and long straight stitches where indicated.

French knot
To work French knots, bring the thread out at the required position and hold it down to one side with the left thumb. Twist the thread twice around the needle, then insert it into the fabric close to the starting point. Pull the needle through to the back, tightening the knot, and bring it out ready for next knot.

The body
Cut out the calico oblong and also a circle measuring 5.5cm in diameter. Place the calico strip with right sides together and short ends matching and machine stitch, taking a 6mm seam allowance. Press the seam open.

Pin the circle into the lower end of the tube and machine in place, again taking a 6mm seam allowance. Turn the tube right side out.

Turn down a 6mm seam allowance at the top end of the tube and run a gathering thread around. Fill the tube with polyester wadding and pull the gathers up tightly. Fasten off.

To make the arms, trim the pipe cleaner to 17cm and glue a small wooden bead to each end. Mark and cut out a strip of calico measuring 18cm x 5.5cm. Turn under a 6mm allowance along each short edge and press in place. Fold the strip in half lengthways and machine stitch down the long edge, taking a 6mm seam allowance. Turn the tube right side out and stitch a row of French knots around each pressed edge. Slip the pipe cleaner into the tube.

The wings
Cut an 18cm square of calico, and also cut a piece of bonding web measuring 18cm x 9cm. Place the bonding web on the wrong side of the calico and fold the calico over it, sandwiching the webbing between layers of calico. Press well, until the web has firmly bonded the calico together.

Trace over the outline of the wings, glue the paper to card and cut out to make a template. Mark around the

Materials
For each angel
4cm diameter wooden macramé bead
Two 12mm diameter wooden beads
45cm x 20cm of unbleached calico
DMC perlé No. 5 in cream 712
Brass wire pot cleaner
One pipe cleaner
70cm of gold cord
Bonding web
Loose polyester wadding
Permanent marker (black)
All-purpose glue (use a glue gun
   if you have one)
Pinking shears (optional)
Medium weight card
Tracing paper
Ruler and pencil
Cream-coloured sewing thread

Trumpet player
Gold spray
Golf tee
Drummer
Polystyrene circle 2.5cm in diameter
   and 1.5cm deep
3mm-wide gold tape
30cm of fine gold cord
Two cocktail sticks
Two small wooden beads
Singer
2.5cm x 5cm of gold card

French knots

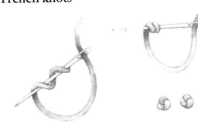

template with a pencil on to the calico.

Glue the gold cord to the calico, covering the marked pencil outline. Cut out the wing shape, cutting as close to the cord as possible and using pinking shears to give a decorative finish. If you do not have pinking shears use ordinary scissors.

Finishing

Take a 22cm length of gold cord and fold it in half to form a loop. Attach the ends to the top of the body either with glue or with a few stitches. Thread the hanger through the head, bringing it out carefully through the wire hair.

Glue the head to the top of the body. With centres matching, glue the arm section to the body, at the back of the neck. Bring the arms round to the front in a realistic way.

Glue the wings to the back of the body covering the arm join. The wings can be glued either with the wing tips pointing upwards, as with the trumpet player, or downwards, as with the other two angels.

Complete each angel by adding the appropriate accessory, gluing it in place. For the trumpet player, spray the golf tee with gold, then glue it to the bead hands. For the singer, fold the gold card in half first scoring the foldline on the right side, open it out slightly and glue it to the hands.

For the drummer, first glue fine gold tape around the top and bottom of the drum. Take a short length of the cord and glue it in a zigzag pattern with the V shapes running around the sides of the drum between the two bands of gold. Glue the remaining length of fine gold cord to the drum to make a hanger, first passing it around the neck of the angel. Trim the cocktail sticks to about 3cm and glue a small wooden bead to one end of each stick. Push the drumsticks into the bead hands and add a little glue to hold them in place.

Variations

There are many other instruments which could be devised if you want to extend the band to more than these three angels. You could, for example, form a small circle out of brass picture hanging wire around a card base and glue sequins around the edge at intervals, to make a tambourine. You could also use the same wire to make a percussion triangle, using a brass pin for a beater.

If you wish the angels to be free-standing instead of hanging from a tree, omit the hanger and cut out a cardboard circle, 12mm smaller in diameter than the calico circle for the base, and insert the card into the base before adding the wadding.

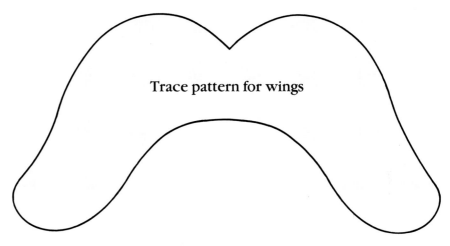

Trace pattern for wings

Trace pattern for embroidery

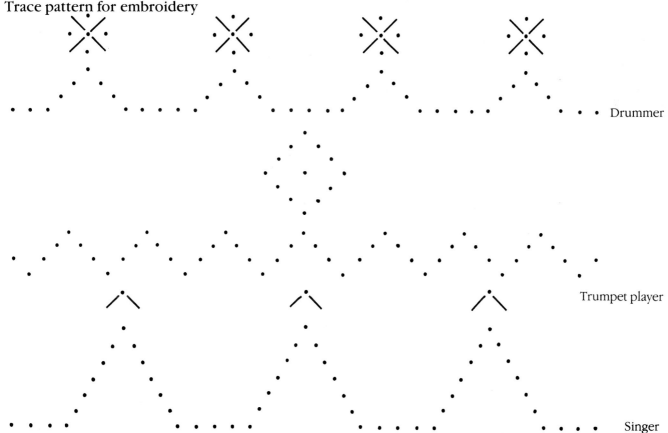

Drummer

Trumpet player

Singer

Clay
450g plain flour
225g salt
350ml water

Materials
Tracing paper
Medium-weight card
Spray glue
Scalpel or craft knife
Red and green food colouring
Silver and gold paints (optional)
Pastry brush
Red and green parcel ribbon for hanging
Clear varnish (optional)

Floral tree decorations

Baker's clay – a hard, inedible modelling clay made from flour and salt – is used for these pretty, Victorian-style floral tree hangings. The pieces are very easy to make – definitely a potential family activity – and the modelling and varnishing make a pleasant occupation for a winter's afternoon or evening. Do not make the decorations too thick, or they may hang heavily on your tree, and adjust the size of the pieces to the scale of the tree. If you have a little girl's stocking to fill, save a small quantity of the clay and model some Christmas fare for her doll's house – a turkey, a Christmas cake or a pudding.

Making templates
First trace the main outlines of the shapes, tracing around the outer edge of the basket and the bouquet and around the outside and the inner circle of the wreath. Also make templates for the leaves and flower.

If you want to make the decorations larger or smaller, draw the outlines to a larger or smaller scale as follows: to make the outlines 50 per cent smaller, first draw a squared grid on the tracing paper, each square measuring 2cm both ways. Take a second sheet of tracing paper and draw a grid, this time of 1cm squares. Working square by square, transfer the outlines of the decorations to the second, smaller grid, thus reducing them by half.

When you have drawn your outlines to the desired size, cut out the shapes, leaving a margin of about 1cm all around each one. Using spray glue, attach the traced outlines to card and carefully cut out the shapes, this time cutting along the lines.

Modelling the clay
First make the clay: mix all the ingredients together to form a fairly stiff dough. Leave the dough in a plastic bag in the refrigerator overnight.

The following day, knead the dough very thoroughly by hand, then divide it into two. Take one half of the dough and roll it out on a floured board to an even thickness of about 4mm.

Using the card templates and a craft knife or scalpel, carefully cut around the outlines and remove the centre from the wreath. The plaits are made from three rolls twisted together. Make as many shapes as you can, then remove the spare dough and use this and the portion which was previously set aside to model the flowers, berries, leaves and baskets.

Divide the dough, allowing a large amount for green and smaller for red, and place it in separate mixing bowls. Add sufficient food colouring to make the green and red of your choice, and mix thoroughly.

The basic shapes make bases for the modelled pieces, and add to the three-dimensional quality of the decorations. Take small pieces of the appropriate colour and use the templates to cut leaf and flower shapes. Add texture and other details by hand, using a knife or the tip of a pencil where necessary. To stick the modelled pieces to the bases, dampen the base and also the under-side of the piece which is to be attached to it with water and score both with a fork.

While you are forming the various components of the decorations it may be necessary to sprinkle the dough with flour to prevent it from becoming too sticky. Use only as much flour as is absolutely necessary and do not leave any loose flour on the surface: brush any excess away with a pastry brush. The diagrams are only a general guide: it would be attractive to vary the arrangements a little within the outlines, so that no two decorations are identical.
Use the blunt end of a toothpick to make the holes in the top of the finished bouquets and wreaths to take the ribbons for hanging. Use a scalpel to cut away the space beneath the handle of each basket.

When you have finished modelling all the pieces, leave them on a wooden board or a baking tray for a minimum of 24 hours to allow them to dry out, bake them in an oven at 170°C/325°F/Gas 3 for one hour. After this, leave them on a baking tray to cool before varnishing, if preferred.

Finishing
When the pieces are cool, varnish the surface with a brush. Allow them to dry before varnishing the undersides.

When you have finished varnishing, cut a 35cm length of ribbon for each decoration and thread it through the hole at the top to make a hanger.

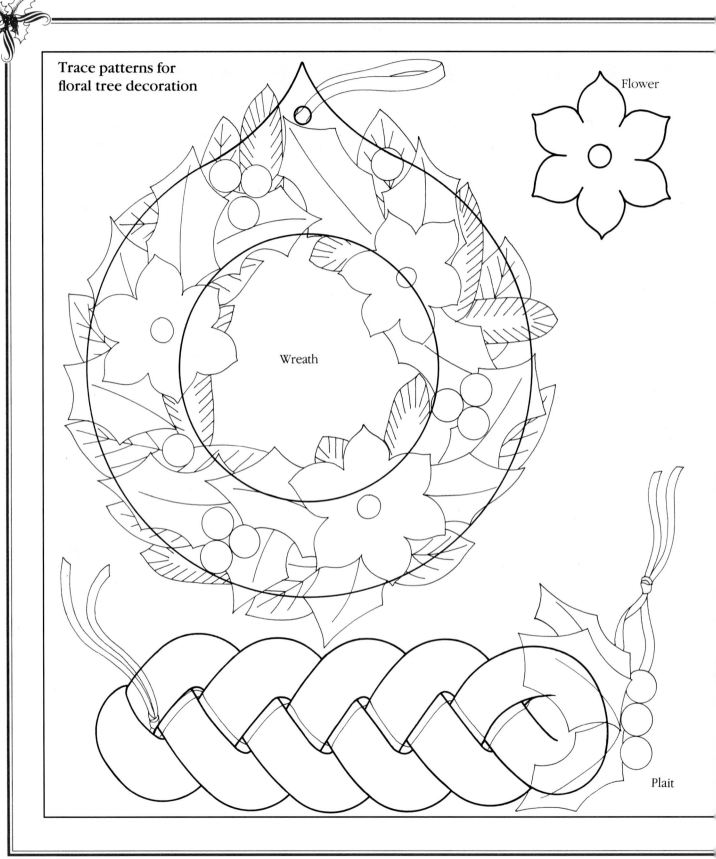

**Trace patterns for
floral tree decoration**

Flower

Wreath

Plait

Fir

Basket

Bouquet

Privet

Holly

Materials
1.5m of 150cm-wide green felt
30cm of 115cm-wide gold lurex fabric
6m of 5cm diameter 8-ply gold tinsel
10m of 2cm-wide flexible gold braid
1.5m of 3mm-wide green ribbon
8 gold bells
Medium-weight card
Large sheet of paper, at least
   70cm square
Protractor, long ruler and set square
Tracing paper
Pencil
Dressmaker's chalk pencil
Gold and green sewing threads
Stapler and staples (optional)

Cutting felt circle

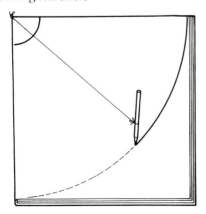

Gilded tree skirt

Plain green felt and gold trim are used to make this simple, elegant tree skirt, with small gold bells added to the large stars to provide a touch of frivolity. The skirt shown here measures approximately 140cm in diameter, though it could easily be scaled down for a smaller tree. Change the colours, if necessary, to suit your décor: a pale icy blue and silver trimmings would look very striking, or for a richer effect, contrast midnight blue with gold.

Stars
Start by preparing the stars. Trace over the outlines and glue the tracings to card with spray glue then cut out two templates, one for the large star and one for the smaller star.

Using the templates, draw four large stars and four smaller ones on the wrong side of the lurex fabric. Leave enough space around each outline to allow for a 6mm seam allowance to be added. Set your machine to straight stitch and sew along the marked outlines. Cut out the stars, adding a seam allowance around each one.

Using a fine needle and thread in order not to damage the fabric, turn under the seam allowance around each star and tack it in place. Turn the raw edges under following the machine stitched line, but making sure that this will not show from the right side.

Clip up to the stitching line at the V shapes, and mitre the points of the stars as you tack: first turn down the point of the star, folding at the machined point, then turn under first one side and then the other. Fold the sides in carefully so that the seam allowance does not show.

Set the prepared stars to one side. It is a good idea to keep them in a separate plastic bag so that they receive as little handling as possible before they are attached to the skirt – many lurex fabrics tend to fray easily.

If your fabric is very frayable, it might be safer to attach the stars with machine-worked zigzag stitch, using a gold-coloured sewing thread or alternatively a thread chosen to match the felt. In this case, you could iron dress-weight fabric stiffener to the backs of the star shapes before you cut them out, which would hold the threads and prevent them from fraying.

Cutting the felt
The felt is first cut into a circle and then the outer edge is shaped into six large inverted scallops.

Start by trimming the felt to measure 140cm square, then take the dressmaker's chalk pencil and attach a length of string to this. Knot the other end of the string: the length between the marking pencil and the knot should measure 70cm. Fold the fabric in half and then in half again to find the centre. Holding the knot at the centre of the fabric, draw an arc on the folded fabric, then tie the string again, to leave a length of 10cm between the pencil and the knot and draw a second arc on the fabric. Cut through all four layers of fabric along both arcs and open the felt out. You should now have a 140cm diameter circle of felt, with a smaller circle cut away from the centre.

If you find it difficult to cut through so many layers at once, find the centre by first folding the fabric, then open it out and mark both complete circles on the fabric.

To make a pattern for the scallops, take the sheet of paper and trim it if necessary to make it 70cm square. Check the corners with a set square to make sure that they are right angles. From one corner draw a line on the paper at an angle of 60°. Take string and an ordinary pencil, the string knotted to leave a 70cm length. Holding the knot at the corner with the marked angle, draw an arc from the marked line to the edge of the paper, to make a shape which will be a

sixth of the felt circle. Cut out this pattern piece.

Lay the felt flat and place the pattern on it so that only the curve of the arc lies over the fabric and the ends of the curve lie exactly on the edge of the felt circle. Using the dressmaker's pencil, mark around the pattern, making one scallop shape on the fabric. Move the pattern round and mark a second scallop, starting from one end of the first. Move around the circle until you have marked six scallops.

Cut out the scallop shapes, then cut through the centre of one scallop to the inner circle.

Attaching the trims
First tack and then machine the braid around the edge of the skirt, using straight stitch and sewing along each side of the braid, as close to the edge as possible. The braid should be positioned 7cm in from the outer edge, following the line of the scallops. Make a neat fold at the beginning and end of each scallop, to carry the braid smoothly around. Start and finish at the edges of the slit, folding the raw ends of the braid under, to neaten them.

Next pin the stars randomly but evenly spaced on the skirt, then tack

Continue the tinsel and gold theme through your tree decorations simply by decorating the branches with baubles and stars. Using the smaller template, cut the stars from gold card, and make hanging loops using a needle and fine gold thread.

Trace patterns for stars

Small star

Large star

them in place: begin by making large tacking stitches out towards the points, starting in the centre. Do not make knots at the centre, but leave a long tail of thread, work out to one point, then re-thread the needle at the centre and tack out to the opposite point. When you have tacked from the centre, tack around the edge of each star, about 4mm from the fold.

Using matching gold sewing thread appliqué the stars to the felt with very tiny blind stitches, taking the needle first into the felt and then exactly into the folded edge of the star. Check frequently to make sure that no stitches show, and make several small stitches at points which have been clipped to the seamline. When all the stars are attached, carefully remove all tacking threads.

Cut the green ribbon into four equal lengths. Take a length of ribbon

and thread it down and up through the centre of one large star, leaving two equal lengths of ribbon at the front. Thread a gold bell on to each ribbon and then tie the ends into a knot to hold the bells firm. Form the ends of the ribbon into a bow, and catch the bow into position with a few small stitches. Repeat, to attach bells and bows to the centre of each of the other large stars.

Starting at the slit, staple tinsel around the inner curve of the tree skirt, then around the outer, scalloped edge. A staple applied about every 8cm will be sufficient to hold the tinsel in place. If you do not have a stapler, attach the tinsel with green thread, running long stitches around the under side of the skirt and bringing the needle up at intervals to secure the tinsel with tiny holding stitches not seen from the rightside.

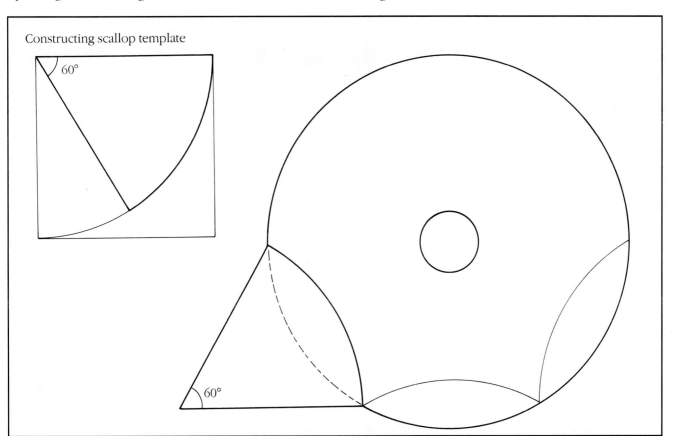

Constructing scallop template

Materials

1.5m of 150cm-wide white felt

3m of 90cm-wide medium-weight iron-on fabric stiffener (optional – to be used if coloured felts are thin and lack body)

6m each of 2.5cm-wide red and green, flexible woollen braid

10m of 3mm-wide black russia braid

Two 20cm squares of yellow felt

One 20cm square of felt each in red, cream, maroon, dark brown, beige, dark blue, grey, dark green, emerald and purple

Oddments of felt in mid brown, dark tan, gold, dark gold, yellow, light blue, pink, turquoise and orange

Fabric glue

Tracing paper

Coloured pencils or tailor's chalk

Pinking shears

Stained glass tree skirt

Black russia braid edges the figures and combines with the white background to give this brightly coloured Nativity scene a glowing vibrancy, like a stained glass window lighted from behind. All the old figures from the familiar story are there – the shepherds, the wise men, the donkey, the oxen and lambs, and at the front, Mary, Joseph and the baby Jesus, with the star above them.

Children will love these simple outline figures bearing the Christmas message, and the tree skirt is not difficult to make. The entire scene, including the russia braid and even the red and green braid around the top and bottom of the circle, is pressed and glued in place, so there is no sewing involved at all. To complete the effect, cut out similar motifs from coloured card for tree decorations.

Cutting out

First draw a grid of 2.5cm squares on tracing paper and copy all the figures, square by square, on the tracing paper grid, thus scaling them up to the full size. Do not cut out the shapes from tracing paper at this stage, but number each separate part that will have to be cut from felt: for example, the crib (1), the coverlet (2), the face (3), the halo (4), Joseph's habit (5), headgear (6), face (7), hand (8) and staff (9). Note

that in some instances, such as Joseph's headgear, the braid lies over a solid piece of one colour.

When you have numbered each piece on the enlarged figures, make a tracing of the finished design, as shown, and write the corresponding numbers on this tracing, as a guide when you come to position the pieces.

Cut out the numbered pieces of the enlarged drawings and, taking the photograph of the finished design as a colour guide, use them as pattern pieces to mark the outlines on the felt. Hold each paper pattern against the felt and carefully mark the outline with a coloured pencil or tailor's chalk. Cut out the felt shapes and either number them on the back or lightly pin each piece to its numbered pattern piece. Try to keep the pieces needed for each figure together – if space is limited and you must pile the pieces up, put a sheet of paper between each figure and the next.

If the felt is very thin, iron the felt to fabric stiffener before cutting out the pieces.

Cut out the shape of the tree skirt as described for the skirt on page 54, but do not scallop the edges. Use pinking shears to cut around both the outer and the inner circles, then use ordinary dressmaking shears to cut straight up from the outer circle to the inner circle. If the felt is too thin, iron it to fabric stiffener before cutting out the skirt.

Assembling the skirt

Lay the white background flat and assemble the figures in position on the background, following the photograph overleaf and positioning each figure 18cm up from the outer, pinked edge. Pin each piece in position. You will find that it is easiest to start with the crib at the centre front of the skirt and then work outwards to each side.

When all the pieces are in position, glue them in place, making sure that all joining edges neatly butt up against each other.

Use the photograph as a guide for positioning the nativity figures beginning with the crib and working outwards at each side.

For your tree decorations, simply trace off the main outlines given and transfer them to black paper.

Cut out the individual pieces of the tracings – to be used as templates for cutting out the different details from coloured paper. Follow the instructions given for making the felt figures but instead of using black braid for the outline, allow the black paper to show between the shapes. Make hanging loops using a needle and fine gold thread.

Starting with all the shorter lengths, glue the braid in position, covering all joins and using it to draw in any details, such as the shape of Joseph's sleeve. Finish by taking russia braid all around the outline of each figure.

It is important to prevent the glue from smearing the right side of the figures. Use a glue gun if you have one, or use a knitting needle or similar tool to spread a light coating of glue carefully on the back of the braid.

The tight curves are the most difficult sections to work. It will help if you stick pins through the russia braid and into the felt, standing the pins upright to hold the shape until the

glue has set.

When the figures have all been glued in position and outlined, apply the woollen braid to both the inner and outer edges in the same way, again using upright pins to hold it in position while the glue is setting. Begin by placing the red braid with the lower edge 4cm up from the outer edge of the skirt, folding the ends under to the wrong side at the slit edge. Repeat the process to put a second circle of red braid 4cm down from the inner edge. Apply the green braid in the same way positioning it 2.5cm inside the braid at the lower edge and 2cm at the top edge.

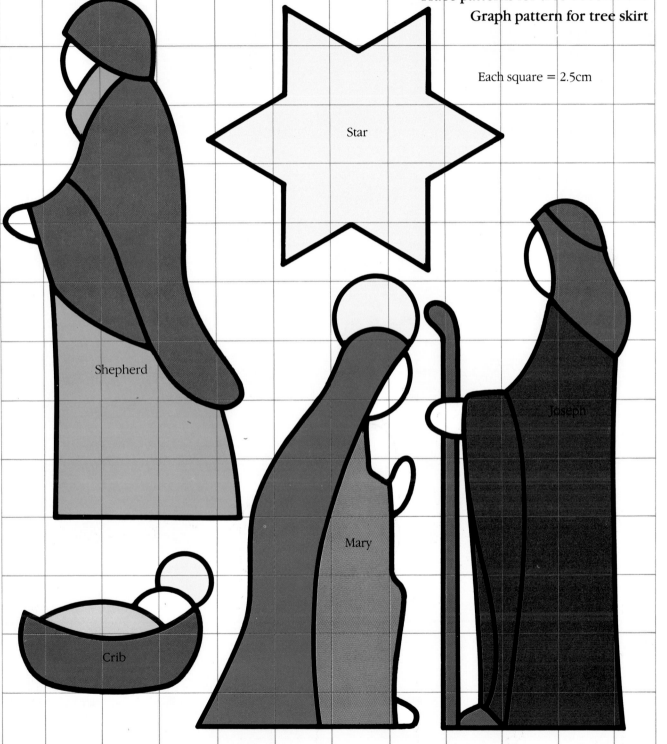

Trace patterns for tree decorations
Graph pattern for tree skirt

Each square = 2.5cm

Star

Shepherd

Mary

Joseph

Crib

Each square = 2.5cm

Ass

King

Sheep

King

CHAPTER 3

We wish you a merry Christmas

The idea of sending Christmas cards was a Victorian invention, a custom which took shape in the 1840s (the original inventor is a matter of dispute) and rapidly became part of the Christmas tradition; for what better way is there, in a busy world, of reminding far-flung friends and relatives that they are not forgotten. These charming hand-made cards make the point more clearly than any commercial offering. In addition to the cards, there is an advent calendar designed to give a stained-glass effect, lino-printed paper, and a set of boxes which would surely be almost as welcome as the presents inside them.

Advent calendar

This glowing advent calendar is based on the idea of a stained-glass triptych window with sunlight pouring through. The construction is not in itself difficult; the main requirement is for time and patience in cutting the 24 silhouette pictures that make up this highly unusual and effective calendar.

Cutting out

First cut out the basic triptych outline of the calendar from black and blue card: working first on the black card, draw a grid on the back of the card of 2.5cm squares and copy the shaped outline of the top, square by square, from the graph pattern given on pages 68-69. Also mark the small windows in position on the back of the card. When the outline and window details are marked, cut along the outline and remove the windows from the blue card.

Place the blue calendar outline on the back of the black card and, using it as a template, mark the outline and the outlines of the windows on the black card. Cut out the main outline on the black card, and working from the back, cut out the window shutters: cut along the bottom ledge of each window; cut down the centre from the point of the arch straight down to the ledge, then cut the curved sides of the arch, leaving the straight sides uncut, to form the hinges. Using the blunt edge of a knife, score the fold line at each hinge. Fold each shutter back and crease it, then fold it back flat.

Using the same method of creasing and folding, make folds between the three arched panels of the calendar on both pieces of card. Make sure that the folds lie in exactly the same place on the black and blue cards, and fold them so that the black front of the calendar will stand as shown in the picture, and with the blue card at the back, wrong sides together.

Silhouettes

On the remaining black card, draw 19 rectangles measuring 10cm x 7cm, four measuring 7cm x 5cm and one measuring 14cm x 12cm, and cut these out. Cut pieces of tracing paper to the same sizes, then carefully trace over the silhouette outlines given for the windows. Attach each tracing to the appropriate card using small pieces of masking tape, leaving an even amount of frame around the edge.

Cutting through both the tracing paper and card, carefully cut out each silhouette, using a craft knife or scalpel. You may find it easiest to work if you tape the edges of the card to a small piece of hardboard, using strips of masking tape, so that you can turn the card around as you cut. Cut out the stars above the centre panel.

Assembling the calendar

Take the black calendar shape and lay it on a flat surface, wrong side up then, following the key on pages 68-69, lightly glue the silhouettes in place. Only a little glue is needed – at the appropriate outer points and the bottom edges of each silhouette – and great care must be taken to position the shapes so that they fall exactly in place at the correct window.

When all the silhouettes have been attached to the black calendar section, cut out rectangles of tissue paper to size and in the colour of your choice. Put a thin layer of glue around the edges of the windows and arrange the colours to create the stained glass effect, as seen in the photograph. Next, put a layer of glue all around the outside edge and along the edges between the arches, ready to stick the black and blue sections together. Carefully lay the black calendar wrong (inside) side down on top of the blue one, making sure that none of the shutters get any glue on them.

To keep the shutters closed, use gold stars, and if you wish, mark each star with the relevant opening date, numbering them from one to 24, using the stick-on/peel off numbers.

Materials

Two sheets each of fine black and blue card measuring 780mm x 520mm
A selection of bright blue, green, yellow, orange, red and purple tissue papers
Tracing paper and pencil
Craft knife or scalpel
Metal ruler
Clear adhesive
Stick-on/peel-off gold stars
Stick-on/peel off numbers 1-24 (optional)

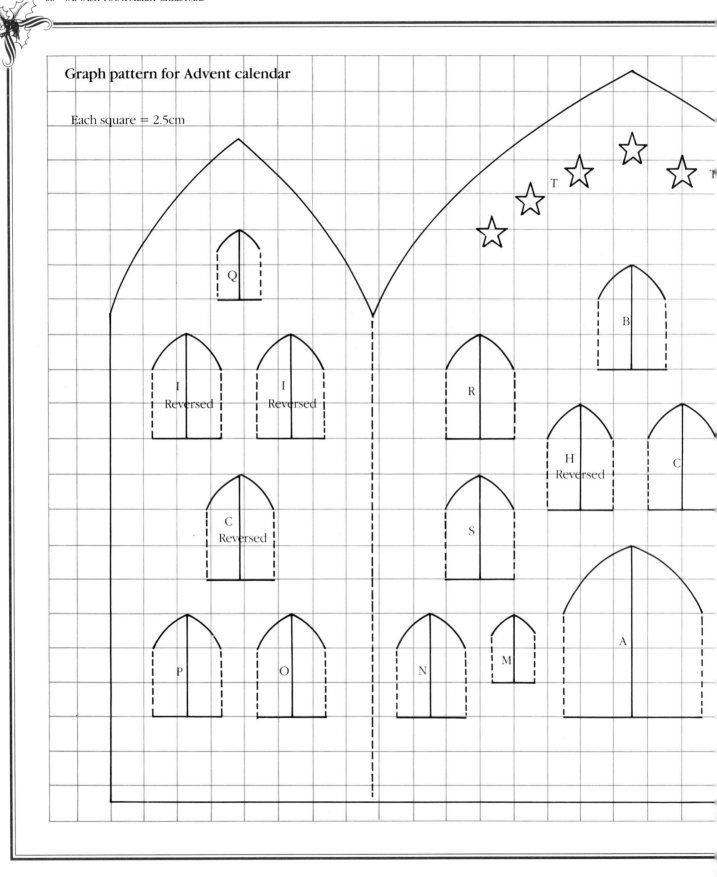

Graph pattern for Advent calendar

Each square = 2.5cm

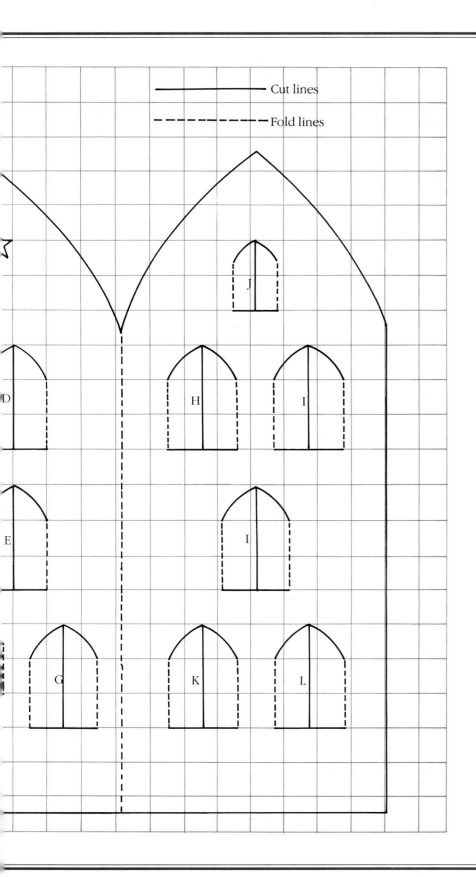

Cut lines

Fold lines

Trace patterns for silhouettes

Window outline

Q

Window outline

B

Window outline

J

A

Trace patterns for silhouettes

Window outline

Window outline

D

R

O

P

N

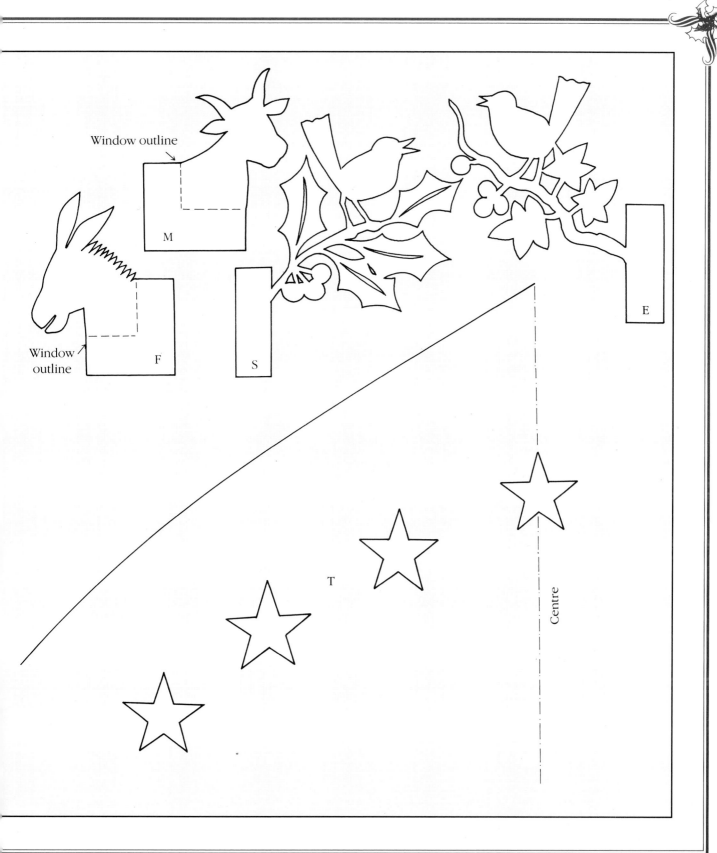

Window outline

M

Window
outline

F

S

E

T

Centre

Materials
34cm x 20cm of light-weight red card
16.5cm x 14cm of white cartridge paper
Tracing paper and pencil
Craft knife or scalpel
Clear adhesive

Partridge in a pear tree

In essence, this delicate silhouette card is simplicity itself to make – all that is needed is to take care with the cutting, particularly around the white frame area where the positive image turns to a negative one. You can make the card in a silhouette form as here, where the white cut-out is simply set behind an open frame or, if you wish to make several cards you could cut the design as a stencil and use this to colour as many cards as you require.

Making the card
First trace off the design. Go over the outline on the wrong side and then transfer it to the cartridge paper, centring it so that there is a margin of at least 1cm all around beyond the outer white frame.

Carefully cut out the design as shown in the photograph, making

Trace pattern for silhouette and border

sure that you leave enough paper to link areas, such as the grass at the side of the picture, the details on the bird or the fallen pears, where the image changes from positive to negative.

Fold the coloured card in half to make a card measuring 20cm x 17cm, with the fold at the top edge. For the frame, cut out a window measuring 14cm x 12cm from the front. Put adhesive at the back of the frame, around the edges, then gently position the silhouette over the back of the frame and press it in place.

Stencilling
If you wish to make a stencil in order to produce several cards, you must first copy the design on stencil board, available from artist's suppliers. Trace the design and then use carbon paper to transfer the design to the board. Cut the design out carefully and then use the stencil either to colour the background (cut out) areas directly on the card or on white paper which can be framed in the same way as the silhouette. Use a single colour throughout or several to vary the effect.

Pop-up Father Christmas

If you own a pop-up book or have browsed through samples in bookshops you will realize that some of the mechanisms involved can be very complex. When money is no object, it is even possible to create a fully formed galleon, with each plank and every piece of rigging and sail rising into place as the book is opened and then, incredibly, all folding away once again. But before you close this book in alarm, our pop-up is very easy to make, even though it has all the impact of the unexpected as Father Christmas leaps up like a jack-in-the-box when you open out the card. Write your Christmas message on the back of the card, or alternatively print it on a small card label and attach it to one of his hands.

Cutting out

Fold the blue card in half to make a card measuring 15.5cm x 11cm, trimming the edges to even them up if necessary.

Trace over the outlines for the body, head and the movement (two sections, one with tabs C, D, E and F and one with E and F marked at the top edge). Transfer the outlines to the red card. Transfer the outline for the face to pink paper and cut it out, leaving the nose to be cut later. Transfer the outlines for the bobble, hands, hat trim and beard to white paper and cut out. Cut out the mouth.

Glue the pink face and the white details in place on the red card outlines, then carefully cut out, making a slit as marked at the bottom of the nose. Stick on the eyes.

Assembling the card

Using the back of a knife or a knitting needle, run along the foldlines – marked with dashes – of the head, body and movement. Carefully fold along the scored lines: fold the face in half, right side inside, then push the nose the other way, so that it stands

out when the face is opened.

Fold tabs A and B forward to the front of the body and fold the body down the centre, right side inside.

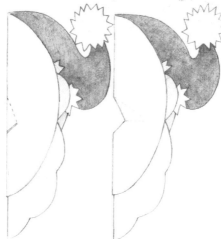

Fold at the wrists to give a little more shape to the completed card, then bring the hands up in line with the body. Glue tabs A and B in position at the top of the forehead (marked with dotted lines A and B).

Glue tabs E and F to the card so that the dashed foldlines lie along the dotted placement lines, with the tabs below the placement lines and the movement above. Glue the second movement section so that it covers tabs E and F and the bottom edge lies on the bottom edge of the card. Fold the tabbed section down so that when the card is closed the central foldline lies below placement lines E-F and tabs C and D are folded upwards.

Glue tabs C and D, facing upwards, to the back of the body along placement lines C and D.

When assembling the pieces, take care to allow the glue to dry thoroughly at each stage before you move on to the next, otherwise they may slip and prevent the card from folding. Take great care also not to tear the pieces.

Write your message on the back or front of the card, or on a separate label, as suggested. Attach it to the hand using a small spot of glue.

Materials

22cm x 15.5cm of medium-weight blue card
28cm x 20cm of fine red card
20cm square of white paper
8cm square of pink paper
Two blue peel and stick spots for eyes
Tracing paper and pencil
Craft knife or scalpel
Clear adhesive

Trace patterns for Father Christmas

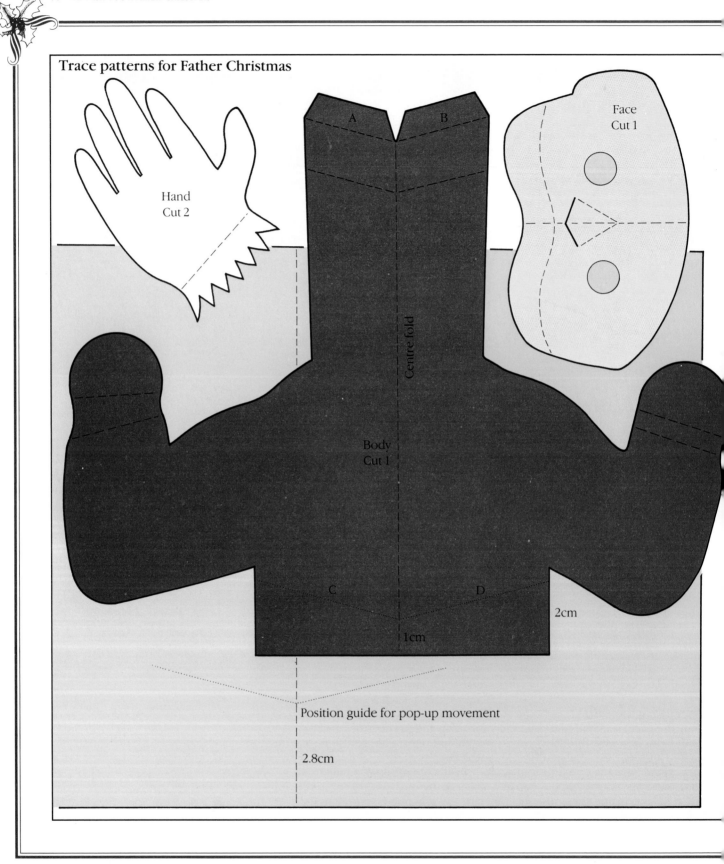

Hand
Cut 2

Face
Cut 1

A   B

Centre fold

Body
Cut 1

C   D

2cm

1cm

Position guide for pop-up movement

2.8cm

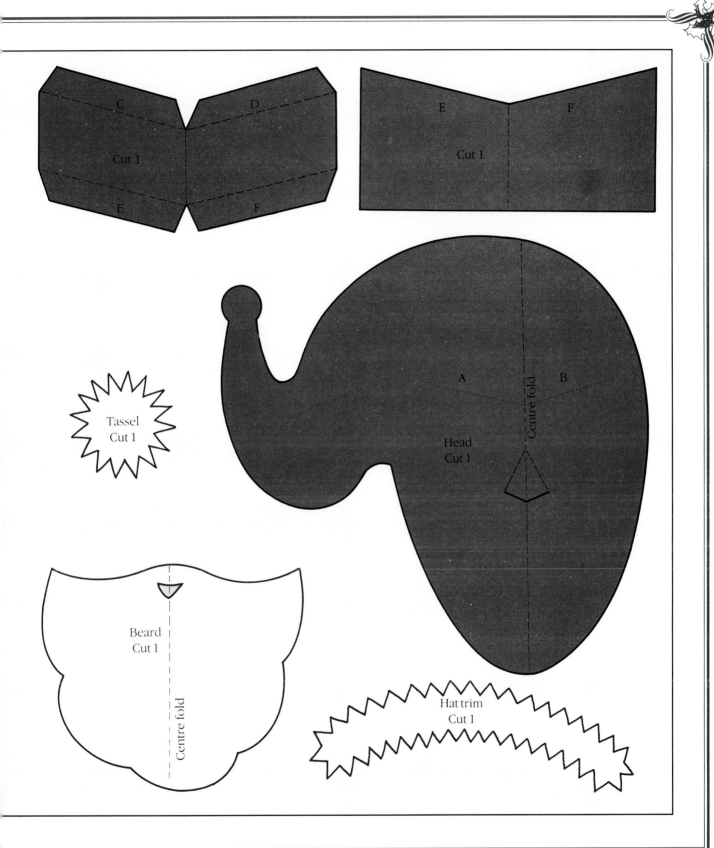

Materials

Medium thick card – approximately
    50cm x 20cm
Thin card cut into 5mm-wide strips –
    two strips 12cm long and one strip
    20cm long
25cm squares of fabric – one of red
    cotton and one of pale yellow cotton,
    also one of backing fabric
Wadding
Light green, medium green, red and
    dark brown coton à broder
Variegated silk thread
Silver lurex thread
Red, yellow and light grey sewing
    thread
Fabric glue
20cm-wide embroidery hoop
Metal ruler and scalpel

Parcel card

If you enjoy embroidery, here is a delightful card for someone you are fond of and for whom you want to take a bit more time and trouble. With a centre in the form of an embroidered parcel, this card is so pretty that the receiver is certainly going to keep it and bring it out as a decoration at future Christmases. The finished card measures 20cm x 14cm and will fit into an envelope measuring 21.5cm x 15.5cm.

Making the mount

From the medium card, cut one piece measuring 20cm x 14cm for the card mount. Cut out the window as shown on the pattern and cut the small label from the inner square. Draw a red line around the label and punch or cut a hole at the mitred end.

Trim the remaining medium card to a rectangle, fold it in half and cut it to measure 28cm x 20cm (unfolded).

Draw the outside shape of the mount pattern on the red fabric, then place it in a hoop and, using light and medium green and red coton à broder, satin stitch the holly leaves and berries as shown. Finish each berry with a brown French knot. Take the fabric from the hoop; press, then cut out the outer shape but not the inner square, leaving a 1.5cm turning all around. Place the fabric right side down on the table, then lay the card mount on top, ensuring that the motif is at the bottom.

Fold the raw edges of the fabric over the card and glue them down. Cut out the centre square leaving at least 1.5cm of fabric for turning, and, mitring the corners as indicated on the pattern. Fold the raw edges back over the card and glue them down.

Using the variegated thread, make a twisted cord long enough to run around the inner edge of the square, with enough left over to make a tie for the label. Take as many strands as you need to achieve the required

thickness when twisted as follows. Cut the strands three times the length of the finished cord, place them together and knot each end. Fasten one end of the cord around a door handle and, holding the strands taut, insert a pencil through the knotted end and rotate them until they are tightly . twisted. Remove the pencil, fold the twisted cord in half at the centre and knot the ends together. Holding the knot, give a sharp shake to the cord and even out the twists by smoothing them, starting from the knotted end. Tie another knot at the fold to hold the twists.

Slipstitch the cord around the inner square, keeping the remaining piece for the tie.

Making the parcel

To transfer the parcel pattern to the centre of the yellow cotton; first trace over the design, then lay the fabric right side up on a flat surface. Hold the fabric to the surface with strips of masking tape at the corners. Again taping the corners, place the tracing over the fabric, then slip dressmaker's carbon paper, carbon side down, between the tracing paper and the fabric. Mark the lines of the design with a pencil or a tracing wheel.

Place the marked fabric in the embroidery hoop and satin stitch the holly and berries. Using grey cotton, couch the silver thread in swirls and loops over and around the motifs. Remove the fabric from the ring and press it with a warm iron on the wrong side, then cut out the fabric and wadding pieces.

Place wadding under each of the parcel flaps, turn down the top corner and then the matching sides and make a neat backstitch to hold the corner. Pin the wadding and fabric together.

Place the backing fabric in the embroidery hoop and pin the rectangular piece in the centre. Backstitch along the stitching line as indicated (this will be the inner fold of the small pleat across the parcel).

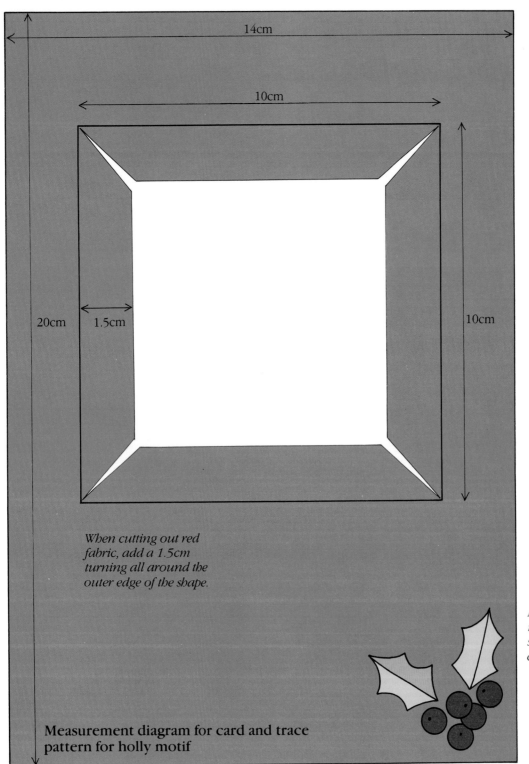

14cm

10cm

20cm   1.5cm

10cm

*When cutting out red
fabric, add a 1.5cm
turning all around the
outer edge of the shape.*

**Measurement diagram for card and trace
pattern for holly motif**

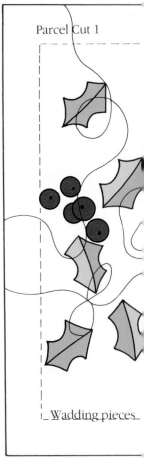

Parcel Cut 1

Wadding pieces

*Medium-weight card
measuring 28cm x 20cm
scored and folded along
centre line.*

Trace pattern for embroidery

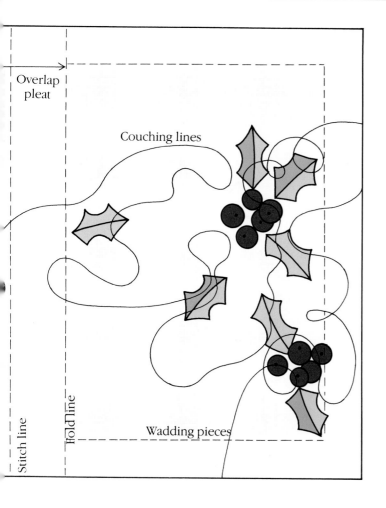

Overlap pleat

Couching lines

Stitch line

Foldline

Wadding pieces

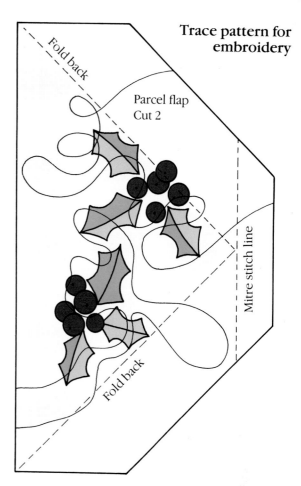

Fold back

Parcel flap
Cut 2

Mitre stitch line

Fold back

Trace pattern for label

Remove the pins and put wadding under the bottom half, then pin again. Bring the two foldlines together and insert the wadding for the top half of the rectangle, and pin. The wadding will raise the fabric, slightly decreasing the finished size.

Pin the flaps in position so that they lie over the square section, with raw edges matching at either side. Before sewing round the edge of the parcel to hold the pieces together, place the mount over the work to check that it will fit and that none of the stitches will be visible.

Wrap variegated thread round the strips of card, gluing the ends to keep the threads in place. Use the two shorter lengths to make a cross shape

over the parcel, then make an unknotted bow shape with the longer length by twisting the two ends round and crossing them at the centre. Place the 'bow' at the centre of the cross and make a few stitches with variegated thread to hold the bow together. Take the work from the hoop and trim the edges to within 1.5cm.

Assembling the card
On the back of the card mount, glue around the edge of the centre square. Place the mount carefully over the parcel and over the front of the folded card, making sure that the fold is on the left. Tie the label on for writing a name or a short greeting so that it hangs just below the parcel.

Materials

25cm square of single canvas with 18
   holes to 2.5cm
30cm x 15cm of medium thick card
15cm square of fine card
DMC stranded embroidery cotton as
   follows: one skein each of red 606,
   cherry 600, greens 943 and 702, and
   white; two skeins each of blue 809 and
   pale grey 3024, and three skeins each
   of cream 746 and browns 400 and 801.
One ball of goldfingering
Size 20 tapestry needle
Sequin stars
Invisible sewing thread
Metal ruler and scalpel

Tent stitch (diagonal)

1

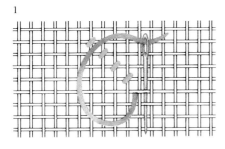

2

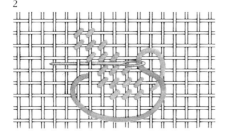

Pudding card

This charming needlepoint card,
worked in stranded silks on fine
canvas, features a highly traditional
Christmas pudding with that cheerful,
rounded shape that comes from using
an old-fashioned pudding bag. A card
as delightful as this is definitely more
of a keepsake than just a card, so this
is carefully mounted, ready for display
on successive years.

Working the needlepoint

Cover the edges of the canvas with
strips of masking tape to prevent them
from fraying.
   Trace over the outlines of the
design and transfer it to the centre of
the canvas either with dressmaker's
carbon paper (see page 80) or using
cartridge paper, a waterproof marker
and a light source as follows: first trace
over the design and transfer it to
cartridge paper. Strengthen the
outlines with a black felt-tipped pen.
   Place the canvas centrally over the
design, aligning the right-angles of the
canvas mesh with the right-angles of
the outer square. Hold the canvas and
paper firmly in position with drawing
pins or masking tape, so that they
cannot slip.
   Shine an adjustable lamp at an angle
to the canvas so that the design
outlines show through, then copy the
design onto the canvas with the
waterproof marker.
   Ideally the canvas should be
worked in a slate frame to keep it
evenly stretched, but you can manage
without a frame if you do not have
one. Simply remember not to pull the
stitching too tightly.
   Work with six strands of thread in
the needle (goldfingering is worked
in single strands) using tent stitch and
working in diagonal rows wherever
possible. It is best to work diagonally
because the horizontal and vertical
stitches at the back of the work help to
prevent the canvas from becoming
distorted.

Tent stitch (diagonal)

To work diagonal rows, first bring
the needle through to the front of the
canvas and insert it to the right of the
intersection of threads above.
Take the needle behind two
horizontal threads of canvas so that it
emerges at the bottom of the next
stitch (1).
   Work the first row from top left to
bottom right and the second from
bottom right to top left. Bring out the
needle at the bottom of the stitch,
insert it to the right of the intersection
of threads above and take it
horizontally behind two vertical
threads of canvas, ready for the next
stitch (2).
Work from the centre of the design
outwards, starting with the pudding.
The danger is that the cream could get
dirty so take great care to avoid this.
Work small areas, such as the dots in
the pudding, first.
   Scatter white spots in the sky (single
stitches) to give the effect of snow.
These are placed at random, but at the
same time care is needed to keep
them evenly distributed.
   The inner border is worked with
two rows of gold fingering, as is the
plate border. For the outer border,
start at one corner and work round
the frame, alternating two rows of
grey 3024 with five rows of cream 746.
Make sure that the stripes are
consistent where they appear to pass
behind the central picture.
   When the picture is finished sew on
the sequin stars, again making sure
that they are evenly scattered around
the border. Use invisible thread to
sew them in position.

Mounting

Take the large piece of card and score
it across the centre with a craft knife
so that it will fold into two squares.
   Measure the finished needlepoint
picture to check the size
(approximately 12.5cm square). Lay
the card flat and cut out a window to
this measurement on one (front) side,

Trace pattern for pudding card

Key

A	White	F	Cherry 600
B	Cream	G	Red 606
C	Blue 809	H	Pale grey 3024
D	Green 702	I	Brown 400
E	Green 943	J	Dark brown 801
		K	Gold fingering

leaving an equal border all around.

Trim the edges of the canvas, still leaving a margin of unworked canvas all around the picture. Place it behind the card window and secure it with strips of masking tape. The finished card stands on an A-shaped base, so the fold in the card comes at the top of the frame and gold fingering cord forms the cross stroke of the A-shape.

Thread gold fingering into an ordinary sewing needle and push the needle through the fine card to make a hole 2cm up from one edge (now the lower edge) and centred. Take the needle through the corresponding point at the back of the card frame. Knot the cord at both ends to make a support approximately 7.5cm long between the two pieces of card.

Position the thin card to cover the back of the needlepoint picture and glue it in place around the edges, completing the greetings card.

Collage snow scenes

Fabric collage cards are easy to make and can be extremely effective, and although they look as if each one has taken a great deal of time and individual attention in the making, they are in fact relatively simple to mass-produce. A raid on your fabric drawer will probably bring to light plenty of suitable odds and ends, or you may have offcuts of fabric from other Christmas makes: the rest is a gentle exercise of your ingenuity and imagination. If you do not enjoy sewing, there is no need to stitch the strips together – they can just be ironed to a base. Finishing touches can either be drawn in with waterproof inks, cut out from felt and stuck to the background or embroidered – the choice is yours.

Materials

Snowman card

Oddments of calico (first fabric),
  panne velvet, corduroy or satin
  (second fabric), and Christmas fabric
  (third fabric)

10cm x 6.5cm of medium-weight iron-on
  fabric stiffener

Permanent marker pens in red and black
  (if you do not have marker pens,
  you may be able to use felt-tipped
  pens but check first on a spare piece
  of fabric to make sure that the inks
  do not run)

Pink and blue sprays (as the card will
  not be washed, you could use
  watercolours and a paint brush if
  you prefer)

Small quantity of green and red
  embroidery threads

Pale green sewing thread

Multi-purpose (fabric/paper) glue

30cm x 15cm of fine card

Metal ruler and scalpel or craft knife

Snow scene

Oddments of cotton with white spots
  (first fabric), white felt (second fabric),
  and silver satin or lurex fabric (third
  fabric), also green felt for trees

16cm x 9.5cm of medium-weight iron-on
  fabric stiffener

White sewing thread

Multi-purpose (fabric/paper) glue

36cm x 11.5cm of fine card and the same
  quantity of cartridge paper

Snowman card

Cut the calico to measure 6.5cm x
4.5cm then lightly spray or paint it
with pink and blue, as shown on the
photograph. Using the permanent
marker pens, draw the snowman
freehand at the centre of the
horizontal strip and fill in details. You
may find it easier to draw the
snowman in pencil first and then go
over the lines with the marker.

Lay the fabric stiffener adhesive
(shiny) side up on an ironing board
and place the calico strip over it, right
side up, matching the top edge of the
calico with the top edge of the fabric
stiffener.

Cut the second fabric to a strip
measuring 6.5cm x 3cm and lay it over
the fabric stiffener so that the top edge
of the second fabric overlaps the
bottom edge of the calico by 5mm.

Cut the third fabric to a strip
measuring 6.5cm x 3.5cm and lay it in

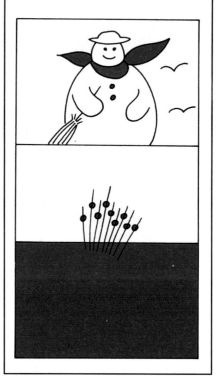

Trace pattern for snowman

position, with the bottom edge of the
strip matching the bottom edge of the
fabric stiffener.

Following the manufacturer's
instructions, fuse the strips to the
fabric stiffener.

With pale green thread and an open
machine zigzag stitch, sew along the
two raw edges of fabric between
strips.

Using straight stitches and green
embroidery cotton, embroider the
stems of the flowers, then make the
red flowers with French knots (the
flowers can be stitched by machine,
using ordinary sewing threads, if
preferred).

Neatly fold the card into three,
bringing one (right-hand) section to
the front of the central section and
one (left-hand) section to the back.
From the section that now lies on the
front of the card, cut out a window
measuring 9cm x 5cm.

Lay the card unfolded, with the front
window section right side down, on
your work surface. Put a layer of glue
around the edges of the centre section
and carefully lay the collage, right side
up, over it. Put glue around the wrong
side of the front frame and bring it
over the collage.

Snow scene

Trim the white-spotted fabric to
measure 16cm x 9.5cm and fuse it to
the fabric stiffener. Next cut the white
felt in a strip 16cm wide and 5.5cm
deep. Cut one long (top) edge in a
curved shape, then glue it to the
background, matching the long
straight edge with the bottom edge of
the background.

Cut the silver fabric to a strip 16cm
wide and 4cm deep, then shape it in
the same way and glue it to the
background. Applying the fabrics in
this way will give a slight impression
of relief to the picture, so that the final
strip will appear to lie more in the
foreground.

Run along the edges between the
strips with an open machine zigzag

stitch and white thread. Finally cut out two Christmas trees from green felt, one slightly smaller than the other. Glue the smaller tree in position, then the larger tree, positioning the latter so that it just overlaps the smaller tree at one corner.

Fold the card in two neatly, then cut out a window measuring 15cm x 8.5cm from the front of the card. Glue around the edges of the frame, on the wrong side, then carefully press the collage in position, so that it is framed by the card. Fold the cartridge paper, trimming it if necessary, and glue it to the inside of the card, neatly covering the back of the collage. This method can enable you to re-use an old card, assuming that the original card was framed around a picture: all you need to do is to cut out the original scene, insert your collage, then cover the inside with paper.

Mass-producing cards

Cards of this type can easily be mass-produced. All you need do is to cut your strips across the entire width of the fabric, and combine the wide strips as already described. Add the details at regular intervals: for example, for the snowman card you would draw a snowman every 6.5cm to make 13 cards from 90cm-wide fabric.

If you layer the strips on a background fabric, as described for the snow scene, you do not necessarily require the fabric stiffener, although it will make stitching and cutting easier.

Certain fabrics lend themselves particularly well to landscape collages of this type. The fabrics used in the snow scene are obvious examples, but others are equally suitable: brown corduroy can give the impression of ploughed fields in winter, black, dark blue or green velvets can be used for hills at night, and pale pink or peach satins can provide dawn or sunset skies. Use nets and polka-dot sheers to suggest snowy effects, and lurex fabrics to add festive sparkle.

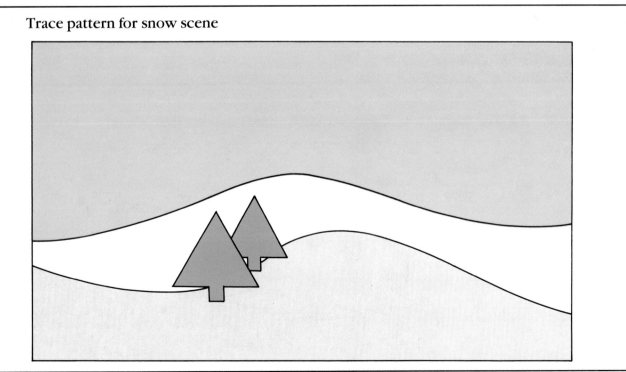

Trace pattern for snow scene

Hand-printed paper

The perfect finishing touch to a delightful, handmade gift is an exclusive wrapping paper, designed and hand-printed in the home. Lino printing is derived from wood block printing, the chief advantage being that lino is much easier to cut. The design is made by cutting away the unwanted portions of the linoleum surface, inking what remains, and pressing the lino block down on the paper so that the inked portions print the image.

This pretty Christmas paper would make a good project for children (they should be at least ten years old, as lino cutting blades are very sharp): the technique is divided into several separate stages – design, making the blocks, preparing the paper and printing – so they need not complete it in one session, and they can learn about this very simple and traditional form of printing as they work.

The equipment needed for lino cutting and the inks are available from art and craft suppliers, including the linoleum itself, which must be the old-fashioned, canvas-backed and matt-finished type, not the vinyl flooring that is commonly used today.

Design

You can use any of the designs shown here, or you might prefer to choose your own Christmas motif. Perhaps you might like to combine a Christmas symbol with your own monogram, to give your gifts a highly individual stamp. Children can also be encouraged to experiment with their own designs.

The printed design is made by the areas which remain after the background has been cut away, so to make the motifs shown here, it is necessary to cut away everything but the outlines. This means that the blocks are relatively difficult to make, but printing is much easier than it

would be if larger areas remained. An alternative way of making the tree image, for instance, would be to cut away only the areas of lino outside the tree and the tub, together with the decorations and the inside of the star, and to leave the rest of the tree and tub. You would then have a solid image instead of an outline, and there would be less cutting involved, but you might have problems in keeping the image clean and neat when printing.

If you are designing your own motifs, therefore, it is best to keep the outlines clear and uncomplicated. It would be irritating to spoil a sheet of wrapping paper covered with several repeated images by having one or two not entirely successful motifs. If you enjoy lino printing and wish to experiment with a more detailed picture or design, you could try making a Christmas card as described below, in which case any blurred or unsuccessful prints could be thrown away.

When you have chosen your motifs, copy each one onto trace-down paper.

Making the blocks

The first stage is to cut your linoleum into appropriately sized blocks. Decide how far apart you wish to space your images and cut your blocks to a size that will give you this spacing when printing (see Printing – below) and that will easily contain the motif.

The easiest way to cut the linoleum to the required size is to mark the outer measurements of the block on the back and then cut through the hessian with a craft or Stanley knife. After this you should be able to crack the linoleum apart.

Before you start making a block, experiment with your cutting tool and practise making lines with the various blades. The blades are very sharp, so when you are cutting try to keep the hand that is holding the block behind the cutting hand as much as possible.

Materials

Lino – quantity according to the size of the motifs and number of blocks to be used

Paper – either fine white paper with a lightly glazed finish (the glaze must not be heavy or the ink will run – obtainable from artist's suppliers), or lightweight lining paper

Water-based block printing inks in the chosen colours (it is preferable to buy water-based inks as these can be cleaned up with water)

Trace-down paper (like carbon paper, but made for designers and available at artist's suppliers – any unwanted marks are more easily removed than ordinary carbon paper lines)

Craft knife or Stanley knife

Lino cutter with wide and narrow V-shaped and broad U-shaped blades

Wood blocks or cotton reels (to back the lino blocks)

PVA glue

Roller for printing

Slab on which to roll out the inks – a sheet of glass or hardboard will serve the purpose

Pencil

Long ruler

Eraser

Hold the ball of the handle against your palm and guide the tool with your thumb and forefinger, with the U or V turned upwards. Push the tool gently forward to make a groove (if you dig in too deeply or at too sharp an angle you are likely to make mistakes or slip). By turning the block slowly as you work you will be able to make a curved line. You will probably find it easiest to work in fairly short lines, removing the loose lino as you cut.

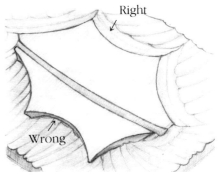

V-shape, using the broad U-shape for removing large areas.

The sides of the cuts should slope outwards as shown in the diagram, so that the printing surface of the block remains firm. If your grooves slope inwards or are too steep-sided the printing surface will be undermined.

When you have experimented with cutting and have mastered the technique, prepare your blocks. Make tracings of your chosen motifs. Lay each block on a flat surface with the trace-down paper over the smooth side and trace over the design. Using the narrow V-shaped blade, start by cutting away on either side of the lines, as already described. Remember that the remaining portion, in

The narrow V-shaped blade is used to run the initial cuts along each side of the final printed (raised) outlines, and you can then move to the wider

Trace patterns for motifs

between the two cutting lines, will be the part that prints, so try to keep this an even width.

When you have cut away all the linoleum surface apart from the design outlines, carefully brush and dust the blocks to make sure that there are no loose bits left. These have an annoying tendency to stick to the inked roller and spoil prints, so it is essential to tidy up before you move to the next stage.

Glue either a small wood block or a cotton reel firmly to the back of each block – you can then hold the block more easily when printing and it is less likely to smear the paper.

Printing

The first essential when printing is to make sure that you have plenty of space (other activities do not mix with printing, which is another reason why it is a good idea if all the family can join in). You will need an area to print and also a space where wet prints can be laid out to dry.

Spread old newspaper (the ink from new newspaper tends to leave marks) or an old cloth over your working surface.

Start by preparing your paper ready for printing. Measure the block that you are using to print any particular sheet of paper and divide the sheet up into squares or rectangles with these measurements, using your pencil and the long ruler, and marking the paper lightly, as shown opposite.

Squeeze a line of ink the length of your roller onto the board. Roll this out, rolling in several directions to make sure that the ink is evenly distributed. Do not use too much at a time – a good test is that the ink should make a sticky noise when you roll it. Check again that there are no loose bits of lino on your block and also check that the ink covers the roller evenly.

Roll ink from the slab onto the raised surface of the linoleum block, again rolling in different directions to make sure it is evenly covered (recharge the roller if necessary).

The layer of ink should be very thin. If it is too thick, the ink will spread and the print will be spoiled. Before starting on a sheet of paper, check on a small scrap that the image is as you want it: if necessary, clean the block and cut away any unwanted bits.

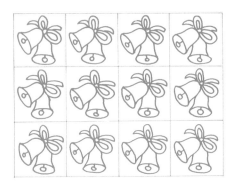

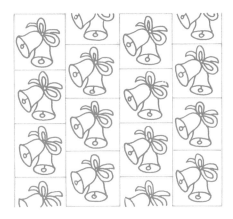

Repeat patterns

To print, simply press the block firmly down on the paper, using the ruled lines as a guide to help you to get your print in the right position.

You can print all in one colour or use different colours. If you are using several colours, for example alternating green and red bells, complete all the motifs in one colour first before changing to the second colour. In between colours, wash and dry the slab and the roller and remove all traces of the previous colour from the block.

In addition to wrapping paper you can also make strips of paper ribbon by repeating motifs in the same way.

When you have finished printing, leave the paper for a few days to dry out. This may be a nuisance, but the ink is slow drying so patience is the best policy.

When the ink is completely dry, carefully rub out the pencil guidelines.

Other ideas

If you enjoy lino printing, you will find that it can be used in many different ways for Christmas gifts and notions.

You may like to make lino printed Christmas cards. Start by drawing the design. Assuming that the design is likely to be more complex than the simple image repeats used for wrapping paper, you will probably find it easier to cut out the outlines and the details, in which case the background will be solid colour while the original colour of the paper will show through at the design lines.

If you do not feel very inspired as an artist, try tracing over an old Victorian Christmas card or a drawing from an old book, simplifying the lines as necessary to fit in with the medium.

For a more complex design of this type, with solid blocks of colour, it is preferable to print in a slightly different way. Cut out the block, but do not attach any form of holder to the back. Instead, ink the block and leave it (ink side up) on the work table. Place a piece of the printing paper over the inked block and gently but firmly rub with a spoon handle, working from the centre outwards. (If the paper is fine and might tear, lay a second spare sheet of paper over the first before you start rubbing.) Do not pull the printed paper straight off the block: lift a corner carefully to see if more rubbing is needed. If it is, let the paper flop back into place again, and repeat the process.

Alternatively, you can put the lino block and paper into a screw-down press, sandwiching it between two sheets of card, and press it for just a moment or two before removing it, ready to print another sheet.

Overprinting

If you become really proficient, you can even overprint in a second colour. In this case, make all the prints you require in one colour first, plus a few spares, then cut away further portions of the lino block and print over the first image a second time, using another colour. The remaining parts of the block will print in the second colour and the first colour will show through in the areas which were cut away in between the two printings. Remember to allow ample time for the prints to dry between printing sessions. The important thing here is to align the paper absolutely accurately, so that the second printing does not blur over the first: this is a technique strictly for those with neat and steady hands!

If you do not want to risk printing in a second colour, you can bring in a second colour by printing on coloured paper.

Rather than printing directly on to cards, it is much simpler to make the prints and then glue these to cut and folded card or cartridge paper.

In addition to cards, you may also like to use one of your smaller Christmas motifs as a stamp to seal your Christmas card envelopes.

Christmas boxes

'It is more blessed to give than to receive' – and these little boxes are such fun to make that you may feel it is also more enjoyable. Taking care to wrap or package your gifts to look exciting and attractive is certainly an intrinsic part of the pleasure of giving. Whether you use these little boxes to enclose something expensive, like a bottle of perfume or a ring, or simply for a delicious treat such as a hand-made chocolate they will enhance the pleasure for the recipient. Each of these boxes is simple to make, requiring only a few minute's cutting and perhaps a spot of glue. The patterns can be scaled up to whatever size you choose, but it is generally best to keep them small and expensive-looking.

Cutting out

First, trace off your chosen design. Cut carefully around the outline then use the resulting pattern to draw the outline on the card. Take care to make the card outline as accurate as possible, and make the pencil marks on the wrong side of the card.

Using the scalpel or craft knife, carefully cut around the outline. Make sure that you rest the card on a proper cutting surface, such as a spare piece of hardboard: it's hard to cut accurately if you are worrying about the table at the same time. Lean the blade against the edge of the metal ruler when cutting along straight lines and cut away from the hand that is holding the ruler, as far as this is possible.

Before you start assembling the box, score along the fold lines with a blunt, pointed tool such as the end of a knitting needle and then fold along these lines.

Read through the instructions before you start assembling the box. If you are in any doubt as to how it works, experiment with the paper pattern or, if you intend to use this

again, make a tracing of the diagram as given in the book and assemble this smaller version as a trial piece.

House box

Cut out the shape and fold along the dotted fold lines. If you intend to use this box for anything weighty, or if you are making a larger version, it would be advisable to add a little glue to tabs 1 to 4, to give the box added strength. If this is not the case, then the finished box should hold together without glue.

Hold the two chimney tabs together and slip them through slot A; close the box by sliding tab 5 into slot B.

Apply small decorative details such as peel-and-stick windows and door: yellow windows and a blue door, for example, were used on the box shown here. Alternatively paint or draw in details. If you are using the box to give a small present to a friend you might like to colour and number the door the same as his or her real front door.

Holly box

This box is even simpler to make than the House box. The basic construction of interlocking pieces is one that is frequently used in box design because of its strength and also, perhaps, because the top is correspondingly more elaborate and decorative than a conventional box lid. If you look at any selection of perfume boxes you will almost certainly find several examples of this type of design.

Cut out the flat shape and fold along the dotted lines A, B, C and D. Cut around the solid outline of the holly leaves, but make sure that you leave them attached to the box by the dotted fold lines.

Glue tab 1 in position, to hold the sides of the box in place. At the base of the box, fold line E inwards, then fold line F, bringing tab 2 in so that the pointed end slips under slot A. Fold along line G, doing the same with tab 3.

Secure the base of the box by

Materials

Fine card – 200g weight
Oddments of coloured paper, peel-and-stick stars, mixed-coloured spots and rectangles and colouring pens or paints (optional – the choice of decorating materials is very varied and you can use whatever you already have in stock)
Pencil and metal ruler
Scalpel or craft knife
Clear glue

The quantities of paper and card required for the individual boxes are as follows:
House box – 30cm x 20cm
Holly box – 23cm x 12cm
Bird box – 23cm x 16cm
Christmas tree box – 30cm x 19cm
Star box – 28cm x 19cm

folding along line H and slipping tab 4 into slot A, taking it over the tops of tabs 2 and 3.

To finish the box, fold tabs 5 and 6 inwards along lines I and J, then fold along line K. Fold along line L, bringing the two holly leaves through slot B. When you have pulled the holly leaves through the slot, fold them down again to close the box. From green paper cut two holly leaves for the top decoration and apply stick-on gold stars around the box sides and lid. Alternatively the holly leaves could be painted green, or you could cover them with green foil, for a sparkling finishing touch.

Bird box

This box is an adaptation of the Holly box, the main difference being that in this case the box is held shut by a small bird.

Cut out the box shape and fold along lines A, B, C and D. Glue tab 1 into position to hold the sides together. At the base of the box, fold along line E, bringing slot A inwards. Fold along F and G and slip the pointed ends of tabs 2 and 3 under slot A. Finally slip tab 4 under slot A, above tabs 2 and 3.

Trace over the bird shape. Cut out and use it as a pattern to mark the outline on card. Using a scalpel or craft knife, carefully cut out the bird from card. As with the box, run along the dotted fold lines at the back of the card with a knitting needle, pressing slightly, to make the card easier to fold accurately.

The bird shape is very easy to make once you are used to the way in which it works, but you may find it helpful to fold a paper copy first, so that you do not risk spoiling the card. First fold the piece in half lengthways, with wrong sides together. (You will see the bird taking shape more easily if you hold the shape with the wings pointing upwards.)

Gently push the tail upwards between the wings along the V-shaped fold line marked A. Bring the other, front end of the bird up between the wings, folding along line B. Push the head portion down into the neck, folding along the V-shaped line C. When the wings are opened out the neck, head and tail should now unfold into a bird shape.

Return to the box and glue the bird in position along the dotted lines marked on tab 7. Put the box to one side until you are sure that the glue has dried and the bird is firmly secured to the tab, then lift tab 7 and fold tabs 5 and 6 in along lines I and J. Fold tab 7 over them, then fold along line L and, keeping the wings of the bird closed, bring slot B down so that the bird passes through it. Open out the wings of the bird to keep the box closed. Stick on gold stars.

This box, like the others, can be decorated in various ways. You could, for example, paint in details of the head and feathers on the bird, using a fine sable paintbrush, or you could spray the bird with gold or silver, masking off the rest of the box.

Christmas tree box

This box requires more folding than the previous styles. Cut out the shape, as already described, and score along the fold lines on the back of the card with a knitting needle or similar blunt, pointed tool. Fold along the dotted lines, taking each fold in turn and then opening the piece out: this will make the construction of the box easier.

Fold along lines A, B, C and D and glue tabs 1 and 2 in place. At the base of the box fold tabs 3, 4, 5 and 6 inwards, in that order, so that the rounded part of each tab lies under the previous tab. The rounded part of tab 3 slips under tab 6, securing the base.

The tabs which form the top of the box are all joined at the sides, but it is easier to complete the top if you consider them as separate. First, fold out the pointed tree sections so that each one faces outwards from the box

Trace pattern for house box

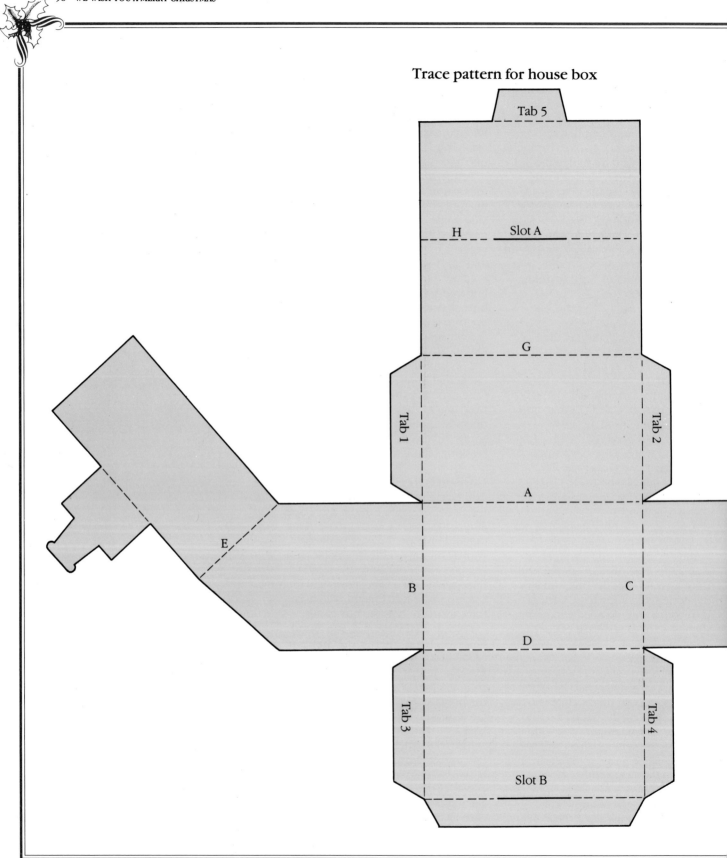

Trace pattern for bird

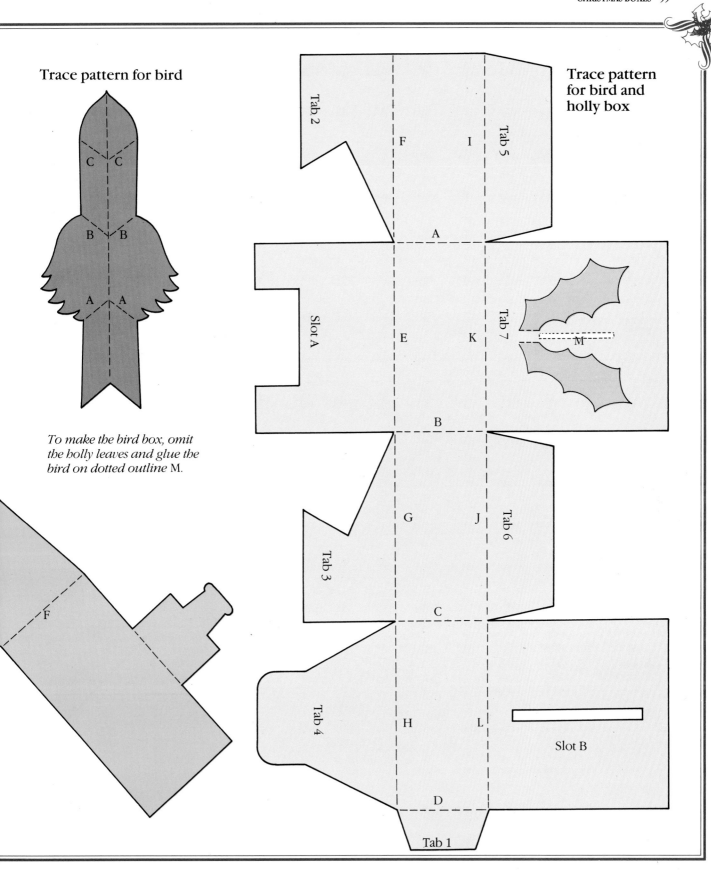

To make the bird box, omit the holly leaves and glue the bird on dotted outline M.

Trace pattern for bird and holly box

Tab 2

F   I

Tab 5

A

Slot A

E   K

Tab 7

M

B

Tab 3

G   J

Tab 6

C

Tab 4

H   L

Slot B

D

Tab 1

F

Trace pattern for Christmas tree box

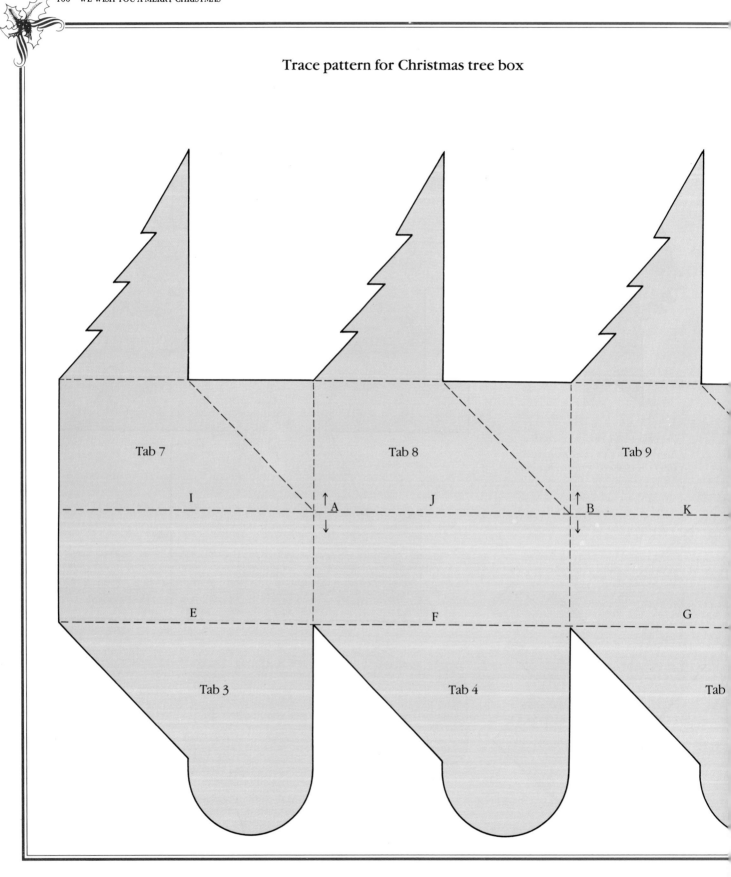

and at right angles to the tab to which it is joined.

Taking tabs 7, 8, 9 and 10 one at a time, as far as this is possible, fold each tab inwards in sequence. Fold along the diagonal, bringing half of line A towards line I, half of line B towards line J and so on. As each tab is folded in, the next will start to follow it. Eventually, when the box is half closed, all the tabs will be pulling each other towards the centre, and each will overlap the next. When all the tabs are folded down, stand the tree sections in a pyramid tree shape so that they support each other.

Decorate the box appropriately, covering the tree sections with coloured baubles (stick-on spots) or small gold paper stars.

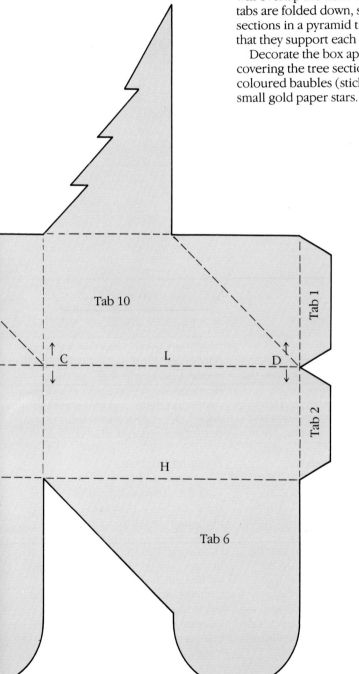

Trace pattern for star box

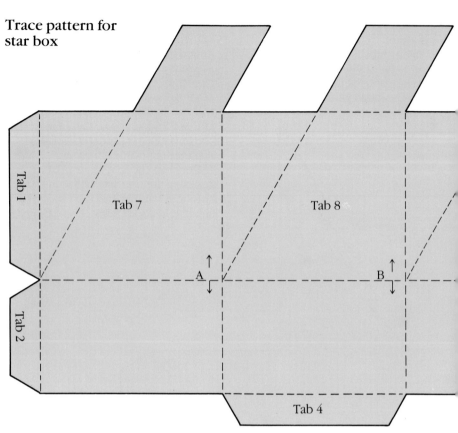

Star box

Cut out the shape as described and fold along each dotted line before you start constructing the box.

To put the box together, start by folding along lines A, B, C and D and gluing tabs 1 and 2 in position. Next fold up the pentagonal base and glue tabs 3, 4, 5 and 6 in position.

When the glue has dried and the tabs are securely in position, start folding in the top of the box. Although the tabs at the top are all joined at the side it is best to think of them as being separate. Begin to ease them into the centre of the box one at a time. As each tab is folded, it will draw in its neighbour: ensure that each tab is folded to lie under the next one along – 7 under 8, 8 under 9 and so on. Tab 11 will fold under tab 7 on the fully closed box.

To keep the box as neat as possible,

begin very gently until you see what is happening. If necessary, make a paper model first. Finally, fold out the diamond shapes on each tab to form a five-pointed star, and cover with gold paper. Decorate the box with stick-on gold stars randomly placed.

Hanging the box

The Victorians loved to festoon their Christmas trees with tiny boxes like these, each one containing a sugar plum or a chocolate, or perhaps a small trinket for a friend who would be visiting over the festive season. All of these boxes can readily be adapted for this purpose, provided the contents are not awkward shapes or too heavy.

A thread could be run through the chimney stack of the house, for instance. You could make a small hole at the centre of tab 7 of the holly box

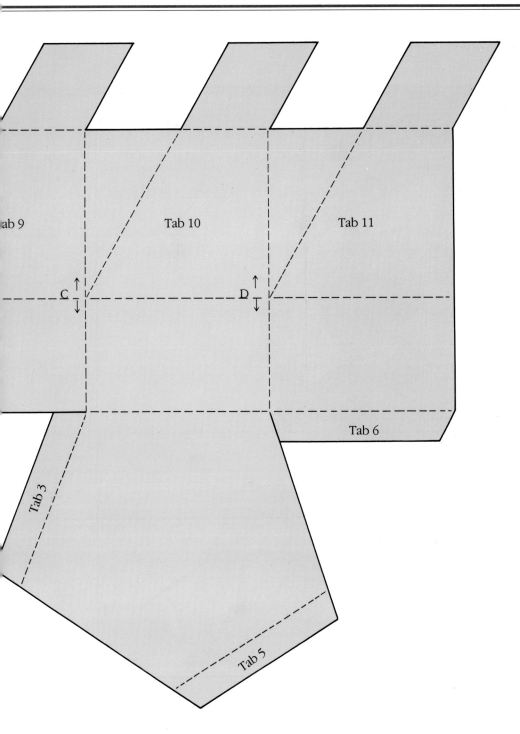

Tab 9

Tab 10

Tab 11

C

D

Tab 6

Tab 3

Tab 5

and draw a thread through, knotting the end to hold the box. For the bird box you could run gold threads through the four corners, knotting each underneath the tab and tying them together above the bird, making a little cage. You could secure the top of the tree to a hanging thread with gold adhesive stars, and fold the star box over a knotted ribbon.

CHAPTER 4

'Twas the night before Christmas

For children, the real fun of Christmas Day begins in the small hours of the morning with the eagerly anticipated discovery that their stockings have been mysteriously filled. Children love to make their own family traditions for Christmas and any of the handmade stockings – crocheted, knitted or appliquéd – shown on these and the following pages, could quickly become part of the tradition of your family. Regretfully packed away when the holiday is over, they will be ceremoniously brought out of hiding and hung up to greet Santa year after year, and there are plenty of designs so that each child can have his or her individual stocking.

Materials

Hayfield Beaulon Double Knitting as
follows:

Christmas tree stocking
6 x 25g balls in red
2 balls in green
Oddments of pink, blue, light green,
    red, yellow and tan
Cotton wool
Candle stocking
5 x 25g balls in white
2 balls each in blue and green
1 ball in red
Oddment of yellow
Wadding
Father Christmas stocking
6 x 25g balls in red
4 balls in white
1 ball in pink
Oddment of blue
Cotton wool
Wool needle
Skate stocking
6 x 25g balls in black
2 balls in yellow
1 ball in white
Cardboard
4.00mm crochet hook (all stockings)

Basic stocking

Tension
15 htr and 12 rows to 10cm on 4.00mm
hook.

Crocheted stockings

Here are four delightful designs, all
crocheted to the same basic pattern.
Each stocking measures 62cm from top
to toe and has a circumference at the
top of 46cm.

Using 4.00mm hook make 35ch.
Base row 1htr into 3rd ch from hook,
1htr into each ch to end. Turn. 34htr.
1st-5th rows 2ch to count as first htr,
1htr into each st to end. Turn.
6th row 2ch, work 2 htr tog, work to
last 3 sts, work 2 htr tog, 1htr into last
st. Turn. 32htr.
Rep last 6 rows 5 times more. 22htr.
Work 5 rows without shaping.
42nd row 2ch, 2htr into next st, work
to last 2 sts, 2htr into next st, 1htr into
last st. Turn. 24htr.
43rd row 2ch, 1htr into each st to end.
Turn.
Rep last 2 rows twice more, then 1st of
them again. 30htr.
49th row 2ch, 1htr into each st to end.
Turn.
50th row 2ch, work to last 2 sts, 2htr
into next st, 1htr into last st. Turn.
51st row 2ch, 2htr into next st, work
to last 3 sts, work 2 htr tog, 1htr into
last st. Turn.
52nd row 2ch, work 2htr tog, work to
last 2 sts, 2htr into last st. Turn.
53rd row 2ch, work 2htr into next st,
work to last 5 sts, (work 2 htr tog)
twice, 1htr into last st. Turn.
54th row 2ch, (work 2htr tog) twice,
work to last 2 sts, 2htr into next st, 1htr
into last st. Turn. Rep last 2 rows once.
57th row 2ch, 2htr into next st, work
to last 3 sts, work 2 htr tog, 1htr into
last st. Turn.
58th row 2ch, work 2 htr tog, work to
last 2 sts, 2htr into next st, 1htr into
last st. Turn. Rep last 2 rows twice more.
63rd row 2ch, work 2 htr tog, work to
last 5sts, (work 2 htr tog) twice, 1htr
into last st. Turn.
64th row 2ch, (work 2 htr tog) twice,
work to last 3 sts, work 2 htr tog, 1htr
into last st. Turn.
Rep last 2 rows twice more. Fasten off.
Make a second piece in the same way.

Christmas tree stocking

Using red yarn, make 2 pieces as given
for basic stocking.

To make up

Hold the 2 pieces of stocking tog,
matching shape. Using 4.00mm hook,
red yarn and with RS of work facing,
beg at top and join shapes by working
a row of dc evenly through edge st of
both thicknesses.
Do not turn and work a row of crab st
(dc worked from left to right) round
shape, then cont round top of
stocking. Fasten off.

Loop

Using 4.00mm hook and red, make 31

ch. Working over a length of string, work 1dc into 2nd ch from hook, 1dc into each ch to end. Turn. Working over string, work another row in dc. Fasten off. Fold into a loop and sew to top of stocking to hang it up.**

Tree
Using 4.00mm hook and green yarn, make 39ch.
Base row 1dc into 2nd ch from hook, 1dc into each ch to end. Turn. 38dc.
1st row (RS) 1ch, 1dc in first dc, wrap yarn over and under index finger of left hand, insert hook in next dc, yrh and draw a loop through, yrh and complete dc in usual way – called loop st–, work 1 loop st into each st to end. Turn. 38 loops.
2nd row 1ch, 1dc into next st, work 2dc tog, work in dc to last 3 sts work 2 dc tog, 1dc into last st. Turn.

Trace pattern for skate blade

Rep 1st and 2nd rows 7 times, 22 sts.
17th row 6ch, ss into 2nd ch from hook, loop st into each of next 4ch, work a loop st into each dc to end. Turn.
18th row 6ch, work 1 dc into 2nd ch from hook, work 2 dc tog over next 2ch, 1 dc into each of next 2ch, work in dc to last 3 sts, work 2 dc tog, 1dc into last st. Turn. 30 sts.
19th row 1 ch, 1 loop st into each dc to end. Turn.
20th row 1ch, 1dc into next st, work 2 dc tog, work in dc to last 3 sts, work 2 dc tog, 1dc into last st. Turn.
Rep last 2 rows 6 times more. 16 sts.
33rd and 34th rows Inc as given for 17th and 18th rows. 24 sts.
Rep 19th and 20th rows 6 times more. 12 sts.
47th and 48th rows Inc as given for 17th and 18th rows. 20 sts.
Rep 19th and 20th rows until 6 sts rem.
Next row 1ch, 1dc into next lp, work 2dc tog, 1dc into each of next 2 sts. Turn.
Next row 1ch, 1 loop st into each dc to end. Turn.
Next row 1ch, 1dc into next lp, work 2dc tog, 1dc into last st. Turn.
Next row 1ch, 1 loop st into each dc to end. Turn.
Next row 1ch, work 2dc tog, 1dc into last st. Turn.
Next row 1ch, work a loop st into next st winding yarn 3 times round finger, 1dc into last st. Fasten off.

Tub

Using 4.00mm hook and tan yarn, make 16ch. Commence rib patt.
Base row 1htr into 3rd ch from hook, 1htr into each ch to end. Turn. 15htr.
1st row 2ch, miss first htr, *yrh and insert from front to back and to front again around post of next htr, complete htr in usual way, rep from to end, working 1htr into turning ch. Turn. Rep 1st row 12 times more.
14th row (RS) 1ch, 1dc into each st to end. Fasten off.
Work in dc along one side edge to form lower edge of tub.

Baubles

Using 4.00mm hook and any colour, make 3ch. Join with a ss into first ch to form a circle.
1st round 1ch, 4dc into circle. Join with a ss into first ch.
2nd round 1ch, 2dc into each dc to end. Join with a ss into first ch. 8dc.
3rd round 1ch, 1dc into each dc to end. Join with a ss into first ch.
4th round 1ch, (work 2dc tog) 4 times. Join with a ss into first ch. Fasten off leaving a long end for stitching.
Pad bauble with cotton wool. Draw sts tog to close top, leaving a long end to sew to tree.
Make 3 baubles in each colour.

Parcels

Using 4.00mm hook and any colour, make 11ch.
Base row 1dc into 2nd ch from hook, 1dc into each ch to end. Turn. 10dc.
1st row 1ch, 1dc into each st to end. 10dc.
Rep this row 3 times more.
Working down one side edge, make 1ch, work 2dc tog, 1dc into each row end to corner st, 3dc into corner, 1dc into each st to last 2 sts, work 2dc tog. Turn.
Work 3 more rows in this way, dec one st at each end and inc 3 sts at corner.
Fasten off, leaving a long end.
Thread end into a wool needle and embroider a line of stem stitch as shown in the photograph.
Use a length of contrast-coloured yarn to embroider ties.
Make 3 more parcels in different colours. Sew tub to base of tree and add baubles to tree.
Assemble tree and parcels as shown in the photograph and stitch to one side of sock only.

Skate stocking

Using black yarn, work as given for Christmas tree stocking to **, omitting crab st edging.

Skate

Cut a skate in cardboard using the trace pattern.
Using 4.00mm hook and white yarn, make 5ch.
Base row 1dc into 2nd ch from hook, 1dc into each ch to end. Turn. 4dc.
Work 8 rows in dc.
9th row 3ch, 1dc into 3rd ch from hook, 1dc into each st to end. Turn. 6dc.
10th-13th rows Work in dc.
14th row 1ch, 1dc into each of next 4dc. Turn.
15th-32nd rows Work in dc.
33rd row As 9th.
34th-37th rows Work in dc.
38th row As 14th.
39th-68th rows Work in dc.
69th row 1ch, 1dc into each of next 2dc, work 2dc tog. Turn.
70th row Work in dc.
71st row 1ch, 1dc into next dc, work 2dc tog. Turn.
72nd row 1ch, work 2dc tog. Fasten off. Make a second piece in the same way. Oversew 2 pieces of skate tog with cardboard in between.

Trim

Using 4.00mm hook and yellow yarn, make 5ch.
Base row 1dc into 2nd ch from hook, 1dc into each ch to end. Turn. 4dc.
1st row 1ch, 2dc into first st, 1dc into each st to end. Turn. 5dc.
2nd row 1ch, 1dc into each st to last st, 2dc into last st. Turn. 6dc.
Rep last 2 rows 3 times more. 12dc.
9th row 1ch, 1dc into each st to end. Turn.
10th row 1ch, 1dc into each st to last 3 sts, work 2dc tog, 1dc into last st. Turn.
11th row 1ch, 1dc into next st, work 2dc tog, 1dc into each st to end. Turn.
Rep last 2 rows 3 times more. 4dc.
18th row 1ch, 1 dc into each st to end. Turn.
Rep these 18 rows 4 times more.
Next row 1ch, 1dc into next dc, work 2dc tog, 1dc into last st. Turn.
Next row Work in dc. Turn.

Next row 1ch, work 2dc tog. Turn.
Next row 1ch, work 2dc tog. Fasten off. Make a second piece in the same way. Join 2 pieces tog at straight edge. Using black yarn work in crab st around pointed edge of trim. Using black yarn, make a chain 206cm long for lace. Thread lace through trim, finishing at top with a bow. Sew trim to boot, matching centre seams. Sew skate to lower edge of boot.
Using 4.00mm hook, yellow yarn and with RS of work facing, work in dc around top of boot, do not turn, but work a row of crab st. Fasten off.

Father Christmas stocking

Work as given for Christmas tree stocking to **

Face

Using 4.00mm hook and pink yarn, make 11ch.
Base row 1dc into 2nd ch from hook, 1dc into each ch to end. Turn. 10dc.
1st row 1ch to count as first dc, 2dc into next st, 1dc into each st to last st, 2dc into last st. Turn. 2dc increased.
Rep last rows 8 times more. 28dc.
10th-20th rows 1ch, 1dc into each dc to end.
21st row As 1st. 30dc.
22nd-27th rows Work in dc.
28th row As 1st. 32dc.
29th-33rd rows Work in dc.
34th row As 1st. 34dc.
35th-38th rows Work in dc.
39th row 1ch, work 2dc tog, 1dc into each dc to last 2dc, work 2dc tog. Turn. 2 sts decreased.
40th row 1ch, 1dc into each dc to end.
Rep last 2 rows 3 times more. 26 sts. Fasten off.

Beard

Using 4.00mm hook and white yarn, make 17ch.
Base row 1dc into 2nd ch from hook, 1dc into each ch to end. Turn. 16dc.
1st row 1ch, 1 loop st (see Christmas tree instructions) into each st to end. 16 loops.

Crochet abbreviations

alt	=	alternate(ly)
approx	=	approximate(ly)
beg	=	begin(ning)
ch	=	chain(s)
cm	=	centimetre(s)
cont	=	continu(e)(ing)
dec	=	decrease
dc	=	double crochet
dtr	=	double treble
foll	=	follow(ing)
grm	=	gramme(s)
gr(s)	=	group(s)
htr	=	half treble
inc	=	increase
LH	=	left hand
No.	=	number
patt	=	pattern
rem	=	remain(ing)
rep	=	repeat
RH	=	right hand
RS	=	right side
ss	=	slip stitch
sp	=	space(s)
st(s)	=	stitch(es)
tog	=	together
tr	=	treble
tr tr	=	triple treble
WS	=	wrong side
yrh	=	yarn round hook
yrn	=	yarn round needle

2nd row 1ch, 1dc into each st to end.
3rd row As 1st.
4th row 1ch, 2dc into first st, 1dc into each st to last st, 2dc into last st. Turn. 2 sts increased.
Rep 1st-4th rows 7 times more, then work 1st row again. 32 loops.
34th row 1ch, work 1dc into each of next 12dc. Turn.
35th row 1ch, 1 loop st into each dc to end. Turn. 12 loops.
36th row 1ch, 1dc into each st to last 2 sts, work 2dc tog. Turn.
37th row As 35th.
38th row As 36th.
Rep 35th-38th rows 4 times more. 2 sts.
55th row 1ch, 1 loop st into each of next 2 sts. Turn.
56th row 1ch, work 2dc tog. Turn.
57th row 1ch, work a loop st into last st, but wind yarn 3 times round fingers. Fasten off.
With RS of work facing, miss 8dc, rejoin yarn to next st and work in dc to end. 12dc. Complete to match other side, reversing shaping.

Moustache

Using 4.00mm hook and white yarn, make 7ch.
Base row 1dc into 2nd ch from hook, 1dc into each ch to end. Turn.
1st row 3ch, 1 dc into 2nd ch from hook, 1dc into next ch, 1 loop st into each st to end. Turn.
2nd row Ss into each of first 2 sts, 1ch, 1dc into each st to end. Turn.
Rep these 2 rows 3 times more.
9th row 1ch, 1 loop st into each st to end. Fasten off. Make a second piece in the same way, reversing shaping.

Eyebrows

Using 4.00mm hook and white yarn, make 13ch.
Base row 1dc into 2nd ch from hook, 1dc into each ch to end. Turn. 12dc.
1st row 1ch, 1 loop st into each st to end. Turn. (2 loops.)
2nd row 1ch, 1dc into each st to end.
3rd row As 1st.
Fasten off.

Make a second piece in the same way.

Hat band

Using 4.00mm hook and white yarn, make 31ch.
Base row 1dc into 2nd ch from hook, 1dc into each ch to end. Turn. 30dc.
Work 1st and 2nd rows as for eyebrows 4 times. Fasten off. Cut all the loops of the beard, moustaches, eyebrows and hat band in half and shred using a wool needle. Mould shredded yarn of moustache and eyebrows to form a right and left side.

Nose

Using 4.00mm hook and red yarn, make 3ch. Join with a ss into first ch to form a circle.
Base round 1ch, work 4dc into circle. Join with a ss into first dc.
1st round 1ch, work 2dc into each dc to end. Join with a ss into first dc. 8dc.
2nd round As 1st. 16dc.
3rd-4th rounds 1ch, 1dc into each dc to end. Join with a ss into first dc. Fasten off, leaving a long end for stitching.
Pad nose with cotton wool, gather round edge and pull tog, but not too tightly.

Eyes

Using 4.00mm hook and white yarn, make 10ch. Miss 1ch, 1dc into next ch, 1htr into next ch, 1tr into next ch, 1dtr into next ch, 1tr tr into next ch, 1dtr into next ch, 1tr into next ch, 1htr into next ch, 1dc into next ch. Fasten off, leaving long end. Make a second piece in the same way.

To make up

Sew beard to face, just overlapping at lower edge. Sew nose 9cm above chin. Stitch moustache under nose and eye about 5cm above nose. Using a wool needle and red yarn, embroider mouth using satin stitch. Using blue yarn, embroider eyes. Sew on eyebrows. Stitch face to one side of stocking. Sew on hat band to cover join at top of face.

Candle stocking

With white, make 2 basic stocking pieces.

To make up
Using red yarn, join tog and make loop as given for Christmas tree stocking to **
Candle
Using 4.00mm hook and blue yarn, make 23ch.
Base row 1dc into 2nd ch from hook, 1dc into each ch to end. 22dc.
1st row 1ch to count as first dc, 1dc into each st to end.
Rep last row until work measures 35cm from beg. Fasten off.
Circle for top Using blue yarn, make 3ch. Join with a ss into first ch to form a circle.
Base round 1ch, work 4dc into circle. Join with a ss into first dc.
1st round 1ch, 2dc into each dc. 8dc. Join with a ss into first dc.
2nd round 1ch, 1dc into each dc to end. Join with a ss into first dc.
Rep last 2 rounds once more. Fasten off.

Flame
Using 4.00mm hook and red yarn, make 4ch.
Base row 1dc into 2nd ch from hook, 1dc into each of next 2ch. Turn. 3dc.
1st row 1ch to count as first dc, 1dc into each of next 3sts. Turn.
2nd row 1 ch, 1dc into first st, cont in dc to last st, 2dc into last st. Turn. 2 sts increased.
Rep 2nd row 3 times more. 11dc.
6th row 1ch, 1dc into each dc to end. Turn.
7th row 1ch, work 2dc tog, 1dc into each st to last 2 sts, work 2dc tog, joining in yellow on last st. Turn. Cut off red.
8th row As 6th.
9th row 1ch, work 2dc tog, 1dc into each dc to last 2 sts, work 2dc tog. Turn.
Rep last 2 rows twice more. 3dc.
14th row 1ch, work 2dc tog, 1dc into

last st.
15th row 1ch, work 2dc tog. Fasten off. Make a second piece in the same way. Join 2 long edges of candle tog and sew in circle to form top of candle. Pad candle with wadding until firm, then oversew lower edges tog with seam to centre back. Sew 2 pieces of flame tog. Using yellow yarn, work a few lines in straight stitch over the red. Sew flame to top of candle.

Holly leaves
Using 4.00mm hook and green yarn, make 31ch.
Base row 1dc into 2nd ch from hook, 1dc into each ch to end. Turn. 30dc.
First side of leaf 1ch to count as first dc, 1dc into each of next 2 sts, 1htr into each of next 3 sts, 1tr into each of next 2 sts, 2dtr into next st, 1tr tr into next st, 3 quadruple tr or qtr into next st, 1tr tr into next st, 2dtr into next st, 1tr into each of next 5 sts, 2dtr into next st, 1tr tr into next st, 3qtr into next st, 1tr tr into next st, 2dtr into next st, 1tr into each of next 2 sts, 1htr into each of next 2 sts, 1dc into each of next 2 sts, work 3dc into last st to form point of leaf, then work other side of leaf as first, but reversing shaping. Turn.
Edging 1ch, 1dc into each st to centre of first qtr group, work a picot (1dc, 3ch, 1dc into 3rd ch from hook), cont round leaf in this way, working a picot into centre st of each point.
Make 4 more leaves in the same way.

Berries
Using 4.00mm hook and red yarn, make 3ch. Join with a ss into first ch to form a circle.
1st round 1ch, work 4dc into circle. Join with a ss into first dc.
2nd round 1ch, 1dc into each dc. Join with a ss into first dc. Fasten off, leaving a long end.
Pad with cotton wool and sew up. Make 7 more berries in same way. Sew candle to centre of stocking as shown. Arrange leaves at base of candle as shown in photograph and sew in position. Sew on berries.

Scandinavian-style stockings

Lovely brightly-coloured stockings with traditional Scandinavian motifs like the Norwegian star and Christmas symbols, including a snowman, a robin or a santa worked into the foot – any of them would make a lovely keepsake, ready to be re-used next year. The pattern is graded for 3½[5½:7] shoe sizes, so if you have the energy to knit two of each you will have seasonal, highly wearable presents – what could be nicer than on Christmas morning to find the companion sock rolled up in the toe of the present carrier?

Note

Strand colours not in use loosely across the WS of the work. Follow the instructions given below for the three stockings, but refer to the separate charts for each design. Yarn colours are shown in the order Snowman [Robin: Santa], and the yarn quantity given for each stocking is enough for a matching pair.

Each stocking

Using 4mm needles and scarlet yarn [royal blue: yellow] cast on 52 sts, evenly spaced over 3 needles.
Work 18 rounds in K1, P1 rib.
Cont working in rounds, beg working in st st from Chart A, reading chart rows from right to left and noting that 1 patt rep is worked 4 times in all.
Cont in cornflower blue [emerald: royal blue] and work 1 round, dec 1 st at end of round. 51 sts.

Shape heel

Next round K13 sts, turn, P24 sts, turn. Using 2 needles, work a further 20 rows in st st on these 24 sts.

Materials

Snowman stocking
1 x 50g ball each of Patons Beehive Double Knitting in royal blue, white, scarlet, black and cornflower blue
1 x 50g ball of Patons Diploma DK in emerald green
Robin stocking
1 x 50g ball each of Patons Beehive Double Knitting in yellow, brown, white, scarlet, royal blue and bottle green
1 x 50g ball of Patons Diploma DK in emerald green
Santa stocking
1 x 50g ball each of Patons Beehive Double Knitting in yellow, scarlet, white, royal blue and brown
Set of 4mm needles, pointed at each end (all stockings)
Tension
22 sts and 30 rows to 10cm on 4mm needles over st st.

Snowman A

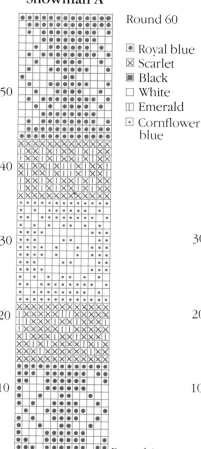

Round 60

- ⊡ Royal blue
- ⊠ Scarlet
- ■ Black
- ☐ White
- ⊞ Emerald
- ⊡ Cornflower blue

Round 1

Snowman B

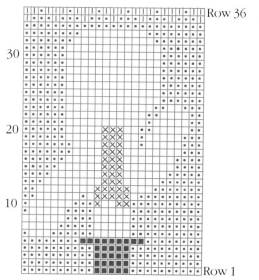

Row 36

Row 1

Knitting abbreviations

alt	=	alternate
approx	=	approximately
beg	=	beginning
cm	=	centimetres
cont	=	continue
dec	=	decrease(ing)
foll	=	follow(s)(ing)
g	=	grammes
inc	=	increase(ing)
K	=	knit
K up	=	pick up and knit
M1	=	make a stitch by picking up the strand between stitch just worked and next stitch and working into back of it
mm	=	millimetres
patt(s)	=	pattern(s)
P	=	purl
psso	=	pass slipped stitch over
rem	=	remain(s)(ing)
rep	=	repeat
RS	=	right side
sl	=	slip
st(s)	=	stitch(es)
st st	=	stocking stitch
tbl	=	through back of loop
tog	=	together
WS	=	wrong side

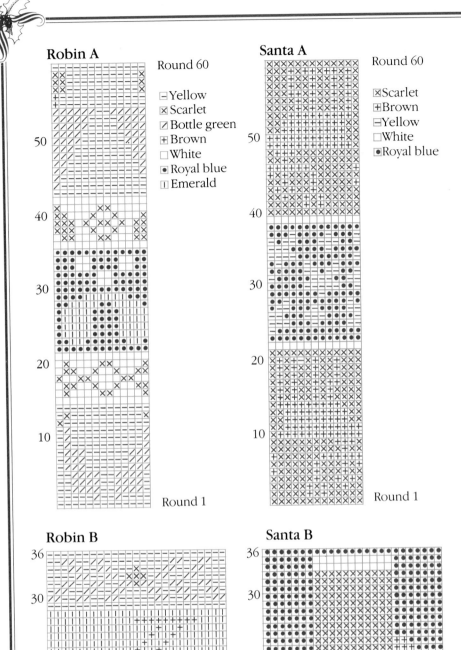

Robin A

Round 60

50

40

30

20

10

Round 1

□Yellow
☒Scarlet
☑Bottle green
⊞Brown
□White
●Royal blue
⊡Emerald

Santa A

Round 60

50

40

30

20

10

Round 1

☒Scarlet
⊞Brown
□Yellow
□White
●Royal blue

Robin B

36

30

20

10

Row 1

Santa B

36

30

20

10

Row 1

Next row Turn, K16 sts, sl 1, K1, psso.
***Next row** Turn, sl 1 purlwise, P8, P 2 tog.
Next row Turn, sl 1 knitwise, K8, sl 1, K1, psso.*
Rep from * to * until 10 sts rem.
Cont with four needles.
Next row K10, K up 11 sts from side of heel, K 27 sts, K up 11 sts from side of heel. 59 sts.
Next row K22, K 1st row from Chart B over next 25 sts, inc 1, turn.
Next row P1, P 2nd row of Chart B, P rem 34 sts, inc 1, turn. 61 sts.
Next row K1 sl 1, K1, psso, K30, K 2 tog, K 3rd row of Chart B, K1, turn. 59 sts.
Next row P1, P 4th row of chart B, P33, turn.
Next row K1, sl 1, K1, psso, K28, K 2 tog, K 5th row of chart B, K1, turn. 57 sts.
Next row P1, P 6th row of chart B, P31, turn. Cont working in rows in patt from chart B, working heel shaping as above until 51 sts rem.
Cont without shaping until all 36 rows of chart B have been completed.
Next row Change to emerald [royal blue: yellow], sl 1, K1, psso, K to last 2 sts, K2 tog. 49 sts.
Cont working in rounds on all sts until foot measures 18[19:20] cm.
Divide sts between 3 needles as foll:
1st and 2nd needles – 12 sts;
3rd needle – 25 sts.

Shape toe
Next round 1st needle – Sl 1, K1, psso, K to end: 2nd needle – K to last 2 sts, K2 tog; 3rd needle – sl 1, K1, psso, K to last 2 sts, K2 tog.
Rep last round until 17 sts rem. Break off yarn, leaving 40cm length of yarn. Graft ends of toe tog. Fasten off.

To make up
Darn in ends and join foot seams.
Turn each sock to WS, fit over a rolled-up towel, and press lightly following pressing instructions on ball bands.
Embroider features on Snowman in black and scarlet yarn.

Robin and the reindeer

Rudolf and his robin companion stand guard over the chimney stack, presumably while Father Christmas fills the stockings. This tiny needlepoint stocking should last for years, and in fact there is no reason why, with care, it should not become a family heirloom to be passed down within the family as a minor Christmas tradition. Its small scale – it measures approximately 22cm from the top to the base of the foot and 18cm across at the foot – together with the care that goes into its making seem to demand that it should be filled with extra special gifts. The quantities given assume that the stocking is backed with the same material as the lining, but you could if you wish back it with a firm velvet for added luxury. Whatever fabric you choose, make sure that it is sufficiently firm and will not stretch.

Stitching the design

First trace over the main outline of the stocking (the finer details, can simply be copied from the chart), and transfer it to the canvas, as described on page 84, leaving a margin of at least 5cm all around. Do not trim the canvas at this stage.

To prevent the work from becoming distorted, it is preferable to put the canvas in a tapestry frame – this also means that you have both hands free for working.

If you do not have a frame you could simply drawing-pin the edges of the canvas to an old picture frame.

If you intend to work without a frame, bind the edges of the canvas with masking tape to prevent them from fraying and catching the yarn as you work.

Starting from the centre and working outwards, stitch the entire design in either tent stitch (see page 84) or half cross stitch, which looks the same as tent stitch from the right side but uses only half the amount of

yarn. You should also check carefully if you are using half cross stitch to make sure that you are covering the canvas threads completely.

To work half cross stitch (see opposite) bring your needle out at the top left-hand side of the area to be worked. Insert the needle diagonally upwards over a single intersection and bring it out one horizontal thread below. Work along the row, making small, slanting stitches; the stitches on the reverse side will run vertically.

If you are using tent stitch, work in diagonal lines of stitches as much as possible, as the horizontal and vertical stitches on the back of the work will help to prevent the canvas from becoming distorted. Remember also to work with an even tension and do not pull the stitching too tightly.

By the time you have finished stitching, the work may have been pulled a little out of shape however hard you have tried to avoid this. In this case, you must block it to pull it back into shape and give it a smooth, well-finished appearance. If the work is very distorted, you may need to repeat the blocking process several times.

To block needlepoint, first dampen the back of the work with a damp cloth or a laundry spray to soften the stiffening agent in the canvas, then pull it gently into shape as much as possible. Draw the correct dimensions of the canvas on a piece of paper and tape the paper to a board. Place the canvas face down over the paper and drawing pin the edges to the board, using the paper markings as a guide and stretching the canvas evenly. Leave it to dry naturally for 24 hours, or more, before removing it from the board.

Making the stocking

Cut away the spare canvas around the stocking, leaving an unworked allowance of 1.5cm for a turning.

Using the canvas outline as a pattern and following the cutting layout, cut

Materials

30cm x 25cm of 10 holes to 2.5cm single canvas (lockweave is the best choice to avoid fraying, or you could use double canvas if you prefer)

30cm of 90cm-wide red satin for backing and binding

Anchor tapisserie wool as follows: one skein each of white 0402, red 0334, green 0257, gold 0735 (only one metre needed), and browns 0418 and 0380 (only two metres of 0380 needed); two skeins of blue 0146, plus a small length of black for the eyes

Red sewing thread

No. 18 tapestry needle

Half-cross stitch

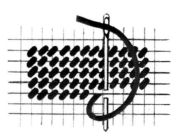

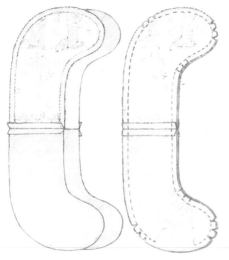

three pieces from the red satin: one piece to form backing for all the needlepoint stocking and two pieces for the lining.

Place one lining section and the needlepoint stocking right sides together and stitch straight across the top of the stocking, taking a 1.5cm seam allowance. Trim and press the seam open. Repeat with the remaining fabric pair.

With the seams matching, place two sections right sides together. Pin, tack and then stitch around the edges, leaving a 10cm-gap at the base of the needlepoint stocking for turning through. Before turning the stocking to the right side, trim the seam

allowance and clip into the seam allowance on the inward curve. Cut notches from the seam allowance of the outward curves to reduce bulk.

Turn the stocking right side out and slipstitch the opening at the foot.

Insert the lining into the stocking and finger-press the top edge.

From spare satin, cut a length measuring 16cm x 3cm. Fold this down the centre, right sides together, and stitch along the length, taking a 6mm seam allowance. Turn the tube right side out and fold the raw ends inside the tube. Bring the ends together to make a loop and stitch the loop firmly in place to the inside back of the stocking.

Chart for robin and reindeer stocking

Key

- White 0402
- Green 0257
- Red 0334
- Gold 0735
- Brown 0418
- Brown 0380
- Blue 0146
- Black

Materials
50cm of 90cm-wide green cotton fabric
50cm of 90cm-wide white cotton fabric
50cm of lightweight polyester wadding
1m of 2.5cm red bias binding
1m of thin piping cord
1m of gold tubular cord
20cm of 2cm-wide gold ribbon
Green, white, red and gold sewing
    threads
Dressmaker's carbon paper
Tracing paper

Greetings stocking

Halfway between a stocking and a
boot, this stylish item of Christmas
footwear is decorated in French style,
with Noël embroidered on the side in
couched gold cording. Wadded and
lined in white to form a turn-down
top, edged with red piping, the
stocking measures approximately
10cm across and 29cm in length. Fill it
with nuts and sweets to make a
traditional Christmas extra for a child
or tuck in small, rather more
expensive gifts for an adult. Although
the end result is so chic, the stocking
is relatively easy to make, so perhaps
you could make a set, with one for
each member of the family, each one
decorated with Christmas written in a
different language.

Preparing the pieces
First scale up the design on to squared
paper with a 2.5cm x 2.5cm grid, then
make a tracing paper pattern, and
include the lettering as well, matching
the registration marks.

Using the pattern as a template,
draw around three matching pairs of
stockings: one pair on the green
fabric, one on the white fabric and
one on the wadding, but do not cut

out at this stage.

Take dressmaker's carbon paper
and transfer the lettering to the right
side of one green stocking piece: lay
the fabric on a flat surface and tape it
down at the corners with masking
tape to hold it firm. Tape the pattern
over the fabric, matching the outlines,
then slip the carbon paper, carbon
side down, between the pattern and
the fabric. Trace over the lettering
with a pencil, transferring the outline
to the fabric.

Remove the dressmaker's carbon
paper, pattern and tape from the
fabric. Using matching gold thread
and catching the gold cord from the
underside only, carefully stitch the
cord in place, securing the ends firmly
in position with several neat couching
stitches placed close together.
Alternatively, you may prefer to sew
the entire design in satin stitch except
for the two dots above the ö, which
can be worked as two French knots in
gold thread.

To make the piping, fold and tack
the red bias binding evenly over the
piping cord. Using the zipper foot on
the sewing machine, stitch close to the
cord, enclosing it completely.

Cut out all three pairs of stockings
from the fabrics.

Finishing

With right sides matching, stitch the green pair together, taking a 1cm seam allowance and leaving it open across the top and partway down both the back and front seams, as shown.

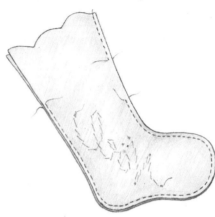

Take one white piece and a corresponding section of wadding and stitch them together (with the wadding to the wrong side of the fabric), taking a scant 9mm seam allowance. Stitch the wadding to the second white piece in exactly the same way.

With the wadding on the outside and taking a 1cm seam allowance, stitch the two wadded sections together, again leaving the top edge and the top of the back seam unsewn.

Turn the white stocking right side out and then pin and tack the prepared piping in position all around

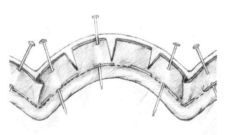

the top edge and the opening down the back seam. The raw edges of the piping should match the raw edges of the stocking. Using white thread and the zipper foot of the sewing machine, stitch the piping to the stocking top, making sure that the ends of the cord are joined neatly together at the base of the back opening.

Trim away the seam allowances of the wadding, cutting as close to the stitching as possible, to reduce bulk.

Turn the green stocking wrong side out and put the white one inside it, so that the right side of the white stocking matches the right side of the green one. Using white thread and the zipper foot, stitch all around the piped opening, sewing as close as possible to the cord to cover all previous stitching.

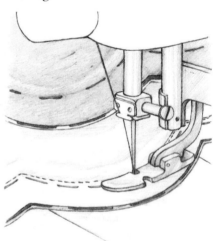

Bring the white stocking out through the opening on the front seam of the green stocking, then turn the green stocking right side out through the same opening. Fold the white stocking down inside the green one.

Close the opening, using matching green thread and neat slip stitches. Fold the stocking down at the top to show the white, piped edging.

Take the gold ribbon and fold it in half. Sew it neatly to the inside of the stocking at the top of the back seam to make a hanging loop.

Graph pattern for greetings stocking

Match A to B to complete the stocking

B

Fold line

A

Each square = 2.5cm

CHAPTER 5

The season for giving

Victorian Christmas catalogues were full of beautiful things to buy but the Victorians knew that there was nothing quite so special as a hand-made gift. The selection in this chapter includes knitwear for children, a charming outfit for the Christmas cook and a variety of smaller gifts, such as painted wooden spoons and a Christmas tree cushion worked in appliqué, to take with you when visiting. Decorating with spices – a traditional Austrian folk art – and making iced gingernut figures are just two of the crafts in this chapter that would make ideal pre-Christmas activities for the entire family.

Materials

40cm of 90cm-wide white cotton fabric
20cm square of red cotton fabric with
   white dots
17cm square of green cotton fabric
30cm square of lightweight polyester
   wadding
Oddment of gold fabric (for star)
1.2cm of 3cm wide plain red binding (if
   you cannot find binding in the right
   colour, buy red cotton fabric and join
   strips cut on the bias to make up the
   required length)
1.2m of piping cord
1m of 5mm-wide red ribbon
90cm of 1cm-wide gold ribbon,
   edged with green
80cm of 5mm-wide green ribbon
Red, white, black, gold and green sewing
   cotton
6 Christmas tree bells
30cm square cushion pad

Tree cushion

Light, bright and frivolous – this charming little appliquéd cushion with its added bells and tiny ribbon bows can be joined to a scatter of cushions on a chair or sofa to make an instant Christmas set piece. Its delightful impracticality and 'just-for-today' air would make it an ideal gift to take as an extra for your hostess if you are visiting on Christmas day, and the perfect accompaniment to a more sober present. The finished cushion cover measures approximately 29cm square, with binding, and the appliquéd tree and star are machined on, though they could equally well be stitched by hand, if you prefer.
You will also need tracing paper, ruler and pencil for making the templates

Cutting out

From the white fabric, cut one piece measuring 30cm square for the front and two pieces measuring 18.5cm x 30cm for the back of the cover. Check that the wadding is the same size as the front cover piece and trim if necessary.

Trace off the outlines of the tree, tub and star, given on page 127, drawing each shape separately so that there is no overlap, then cut them out from the tracing paper.

Use the tracing paper templates to mark and cut out a tree from green fabric and tub from white fabric. Whether you intend to stitch the appliqué by hand or with machine satin stitch, you should add an allowance of 5mm all around each piece.

Gold fabric is often very easily frayed, so do not cut out the star at this stage but mark the outline on the fabric with a pencil and then cut out around the shape, approximately 1cm outside the points of the star. You may find that it helps if you iron the piece on to a scrap of fabric stiffener to hold the threads securely and then cut out the shape.

When you are ready to attach the motifs to the cover (see below), pin and tack the shapes in place, without trimming off the allowance; either machine zigzag stitch along the marked outline and then trim the excess fabric away, using sharp embroidery scissors and cutting as close as possible to the stitching line, or turn under a 5mm turning, and hand sew using buttonhole stitch.

Making the appliqué

Pin the tub and tree in position on the red square. To avoid wrinkles, make sure that all the pieces are absolutely flat, ironing them if necessary. Tack each piece thoroughly, tacking about 6mm in from the raw edge, then press the work again.

Set your machine to a narrow satin stitch (close zigzag) and machine the tree and tub in position, using matching green thread for the tree and white for the tub. Trim away the surplus fabric beyond the stitching and remove the tacking.

Using green thread and small straight stitches, make the zigzag decorative lines on the tub. Still using green thread and straight stitch, take the white front cover section and decorate it with diagonal lines of green stitching, set 2cm apart.

Using black thread, stitch in the trunk of the tree, either with short lines of machine straight stitch, set very close together, or with hand-sewn stitches.

Centre the red appliquéd square over the front cover, with the wrong side of the appliqué to the right side of the cover. Pin and tack thoroughly, all around the edges. Cut the green ribbon into four 19cm strips. Tuck under one end of each strip for 5mm and lay the strips in a square, framing the appliqué design. Position the strips so that each neatened edge covers the raw edge of another strip. Using green thread and straight stitch, sew the ribbon in position, sewing along each long side, close to the edge, and across the ends.

Cut the gold ribbon into four 21cm strips and repeat the process, making sure that the gold ribbon butts up against the green.

Tack the star in position over the ribbon borders and sew it in place using gold thread and satin stitch.

Finishing the cover

Take the two pieces of white cotton fabric for the back of the cover and hem one long side of each: turn under 1cm and press, then turn under another 2.5cm and press again; using white cotton and straight stitch, sew the fold in position, stitching close to the inner folded edge.

Lap the wrong side of one piece over the right side of the other, so that the first just covers the stitching line of the second. Stitching 1cm in from the raw edges at either end of the hems, stitch across to hold the overlap in position. The joined pieces should now be the same size as the front cover.

Fold the red binding over the piping cord and, using red thread and the zipper foot of the sewing machine, stitch close to the cord so that it is enclosed in the binding. Next take the front cover and lay the wadding on the wrong side of it. Pin and tack around the edges, then stitch the wadding to the back of the cover, stitching 9mm (just under 1cm) in from the raw edges. Lay the piping on the right side of the cover, with the raw edges of the piping matching the raw edges of the cover. Pin and tack in position, clipping into the seam allowances of the piping at the corners as necessary.

Where the two ends of piping meet (this should not be at a corner) they should overlap for about 2.5cm. Unpick the casing at each end and join the edges with a diagonal seam. Unravel the strands of the cord for the length of the overlap. Cut away two strands from one end and one strand from the other to reduce bulk. Twist

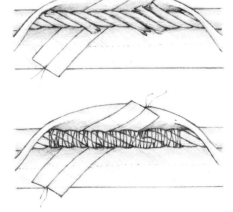

the remaining strands together and bind them securely with thread. Do not pull the cord too tightly or the ends will work apart in wear. Fold the casing back over the cord.

Again using the zipper foot and red thread, stitch the piping to the front cover.

Lay the back cover over the front cover, with right sides together and stitch around the edge. Stitch as close to the piping as possible, to cover the previous row on stitching. Snip V-shapes into the seam allowances at the corners and turn the cover through to the right side.

Stitch the bells in position, stitching through the front cover only. Cut the red ribbon into six equal lengths. Fold each strip into a bow shape, but do not knot them: stitch them in position with red thread so that the thread forms the ribbons into bows and secures them to the front of the cover.

Measurement diagram for tree cushion

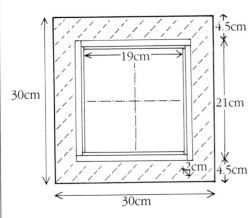

Trace pattern for tree cushion motif

Materials

Star aniseed
Cloves
Cinnamon (one stick)
Juniper berries
White peppercorns
Sprigs of dried ruscus (available from florists)
Silver stem wire
Tying wire
Brown stem binding tape
6 small pearl beads
20cm of fine gold cord
40cm of fine gold bullion
40cm of thick gold bullion
50cm of gold russia braid
30cm of 1cm-wide brown ribbon, edged with gold
Gold spray
25cm x 15cm of medium-weight brown card
Tracing paper and pencil
Craft knife or scalpel
Clear adhesive
Hot glue

Spicy heart

This fragrant, spicy heart, decorated with cloves, cinnamon, juniper, star aniseed and peppercorns bound with gold threads would make a charming Christmas gift for a friend. The making of these spice gifts is a traditional Austrian folk art, originally developed in Salzburg, and makes a pleasant occupation for a cold winter's day when there is little temptation to go outside. The heart shown here gives an idea of how the varied elements of gold wrapped cloves, aniseed and other spices can be used, but give your imagination a free rein and create your own little gifts, decorations, place settings and wreaths.

Card base

First trace the heart shape and transfer it to card. Cut out one heart shape, then use this as a template to mark and cut out a second heart. Use clear adhesive to glue the two shapes together, brown side out, at the same time inserting the gold cord, formed into a loop, at the centre top of the heart.

Spray approximately 60 juniper berries gold (you may need more if yours are small) and set them aside to dry. When they are dry, glue a row of berries around the outside edge of the heart, starting at the lowest point. Use plenty of glue so that the berries are firmly bedded in glue and work in short lengths to avoid the glue drying out before you have finished.

Next glue a row of natural juniper berries inside the gold row. The inner row is formed by alternating cloves and white peppercorns: trim the stems of the cloves as necessary, so that the heads stand proud of the inner edge of the heart and the ends touch the inner row of juniper berries and appear even in length.

Cover the outer edge of the card heart with gold russia braid, starting and finishing at the top centre of the heart butting the edges together.

Decoration

First take 15 well-shaped cloves and prepare these. For each clove cut a piece of thin bullion to go around the head of the clove – approximately 15 to 18mm long according to the size of the clove. Cut a piece of stem wire 15cm long and thread it through the hollow bullion. Take one end of the wire and thread it again through 3mm of bullion at the other end, then pull the ends together to form a bullion ring. Push this over the head of the clove and wrap the ends of the wire around the stem a few times. Cut a short length of brown tape and wind it around the stem and wire. When you have prepared all 15 cloves, join them into groups of five with tying wire and again finish with tape.

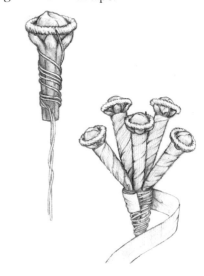

Break the cinnamon into two unequal lengths and bind the pieces together at one end. Cover the tying wire with brown tape.

Cut off tips of ruscus to make sprays about 5cm long. Tie them together in twos and threes to make five small sprays.

Make two bullion spirals: cut the thick bullion in half and thread silver wire through each piece. For each piece, let a short length of wire project at one end and then bend this back unobtrusively over the bullion, to

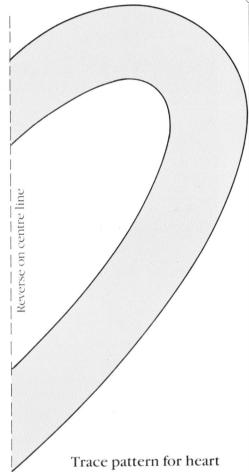

Trace pattern for heart

Reverse on centre line

prevent it from slipping. Leave a longer length of wire at the other end and bind this with brown tape to make a stem. Coil the bullion around a knitting needle to form it into a spiral.

Next make a star aniseed flower (see far right). Start by breaking off any damaged pieces from the star and gluing points into any gaps to make a full flower shape. Thread the six pearls on silver wire and twist it into a small circle. Thread a 6cm length of fine bullion on silver wire and wind it around the pearl garland so that it twists between each pearl. Put the garland at the centre of the aniseed flower and twist the wire ends unobtrusively together at the back.

Assemble the various decorations at the top of the heart as shown in the picture, starting with the ruscus sprays and gluing them firmly into position. Next glue the three bunches of cloves in place, then the bullion spirals and the cinnamon, and then the aniseed flower. Finish by forming the ribbon into four loops, with 6cm ends, and glue this in place to complete the heart.

Star aniseed

Christmas tree jumper

Here is a quick and simple way for a non-knitter to give a plain purchased sweater a festive air that is bound to delight the smaller branches of the family tree. The tree or other motifs are embroidered onto the sweater using the technique demonstrated here, which is known as Swiss darning. Originally a way of reinforcing threadbare woollens, it is now often used to decorate stocking stitch fabric by covering the stitches one by one, using lengths of coloured yarn of an identical quality and thickness to that used in the knitting. For extra fun on the great day, you can add coloured beads and star-shaped sequins to the trees – if they make the sweater look too specifically intended for Christmas they can always be taken off when the big tree is also stripped of its decorations. The tree motif is shown here on a sweater, but of course any piece of knitwear could be used as a base for your chosen motif, provided it is knitted in stocking stitch.

Swiss-darned motifs

The motifs are worked by copying the chart. Each square on the chart represents one stitch on the knitted fabric. Since knitted stitches are rectangular rather than square, the motif on the knitted fabric will appear rather more flattened than it does on the chart, so do not worry if your chart motif seems to be slightly elongated and distorted.

The positioning of the motifs and the number of repetitions is up to you. You may find that it helps to make small paper cut-outs and pin these to the garment, moving them around until you have a satisfactory arrangement.

Use each colour separately, working as much as possible from right to left and then from left to right, to keep the back of the work neat and smooth. Keep an even tension while stitching, taking particular care not to pull the

yarn too tightly. Finish off the ends at the back of the work by threading them through two or three stitches before cutting off the surplus yarn.

The darning

1 Thread a blunt-ended wool needle with the chosen yarn and begin at the lower right-hand corner of the motif to be worked. Secure the end of the yarn at the back of the work by running it under several stitches. Bring the yarn through to the front through the base of the first stitch to be covered. Insert the needle from right to left behind the stitch above.

2 Pull the yarn through. Insert the needle through the base of the stitch and bring out through the base of the next stitch to the left.

3 Pull the yarn through, thus covering the first stitch. Continue in this way across the row, covering each stitch in turn and working from right to left.
4 Work the next row of stitches above the first, working from left to right, as shown.

Materials
Purchased knitwear
Oddments of wool in the same quality and thickness as the garment (if this is knitted in pure wool, and will not be washed too frequently, you may find that tapestry wools are an economical option)
Beads and sequins (optional – for tree decorations)
Blunt-ended wool needle

Chart for Swiss-darned tree motif

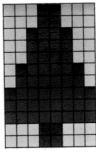

Each motif runs across 8 sts at its widest point and down 12 rows.

Materials

Patons Diploma DK as follows:

Complete set
6 x 50g balls in red (A)
1 x 50g ball in green (B)
1 x 50g ball in white (C)
1 pair each of 3mm and 3¾mm needles
2.50mm crochet hook (scarf only)
45 beads or small buttons for berries

Scarf
4 x 50g balls in red (A)
1 x 50g ball in green (B)
1 x 50g ball in white (C)
18 beads

Hat
2 x 50g balls in red (A)
1 x 50g ball in green (B)
1 x 50g ball in white (C)
21 beads

Mittens
1 x 50g ball in red (A)
1 x 50g ball in green (B)
1 x 50g ball in white (C)
6 beads

Note
When working the snowflake patt, use a separate length of yarn for each dot. When changing colours for dots, twist yarns on WS to avoid holes.

Tension
24 sts and 32 rows to 10cm on 3¾mm needles over st st.

Christmas knits

In bygone days, every member of the household would be given a new outfit at Christmas-time, and children love to benefit from this tradition, especially when the new clothes are as bright and colourful as this delightful set of scarf, hat and mittens. The scarf measures approximately 23cm by 115cm and the hat and mittens are in three sizes, to fit a 5[6:7] year old. All

are fairly quick and easy to knit.

Scarf

Using smaller needles and A, cast on
54 sts. Work 8 rows in garter stitch (K
every row).

Change to larger needles, beg with a K
row and work 6 rows in st st.
Beg working holly patt as foll:
1st row (K8A, K8B) 3 times, K6A.
2nd row P6A, (P8B, P8A) 3 times.
3rd row (K8A, K4B, K2A, K2B) 3 times,

K6A.

4th row P6A, (P2B, P2A, P4B, K8A) 3 times.

These 4 rows set the holly patt. Cont working in this way from chart beg with 5th row until 14 rows have been completed.

Break off B.

Work 6 rows in st st using A only.

Beg working snowflake patt as foll:

1st row K6A, *K2C, K8A, rep from * to last 8 sts, K2C, K6A.

2nd row P5A, *P4C, P6A, rep from * to last 9 sts, P4C, P5A.

3rd row K5A, *K4C, K6A, rep from * to last 9 sts, K4C, K5A.

4th row P6A, *P2C, P8A, rep from * to last 8 sts, P2C, P6A.

Beg with a K row, work 12 rows in st st using A only.

17th row K1A, *K2C, K8A, rep from * to last 3 sts, K2C, K1A.

18th row P4C, *P6A, P4C, rep from * to end.

19th row K4C, *K6A, K4C, rep from * to end.

20th row P1A, *P2C, P8A, rep from * to last 3 sts P2C, P1A.

Work 12 rows in st st using A only.

These 32 rows form snowflake patt.

Rep snowflake patt until scarf measures approx 105cm from beg, ending after 6 rows st st.

Work the holly patt in reverse turning the chart upside down and beg with 14th row which now becomes first row as foll:

1st row K14A, K6C, (K10A, K6C) twice, K2A.

When chart is complete work 6 rows in st st.

Change to smaller needles and work 8 rows garter stitch.

Cast off.

Finishing the scarf

Using a crochet hook and A, work a row of double crochet evenly along each long edge of the scarf to prevent curling.

Cut sufficient 23cm lengths of A ready to make a fringe at each end of the scarf of approximately 27 knots.

To make the fringe, take 3 strands together and, with RS facing, insert hook as shown from back to front through the main fabric; fold the three strands in half over the hook, then pull the looped yarn through the fabric from front to back.

Place the hook around the ends of yarn and draw the ends through the loop on the hook. Pull the strands tightly to make a neat knot. Repeat along the length of the fabric. Trim the ends evenly.

Sew the berries in position as illustrated.

Hat

Using smaller needles and A, cast on 113(115,117)sts.

Work in K1, P1 rib for 8[9:10]cm, inc 1 st in last row. 114[116:118] sts.

Change to larger needles and work 6 rows in st st beg with a K row.

Beg working holly patt as foll:

1st row K1[2:3]A, *K6A, K8B, rep from * to last 1[2:3] sts, K1[2:3]A.

This row sets holly patt. Cont working from chart until 14 rows have been completed, keeping edge sts in st st and A.

Break off B.

Work 6 rows in st st using A only.

Beg working snowflake patt as foll:

1st row K7[8:9]A, *K1A, K2C, K9A, rep from * ending last rep K8[9:10]A.

2nd row P7[8:9]A, P4C, *P8A, P4C, rep from * to last 7[8:9] sts, P7[8:9]A.

3rd row K7[8:9]A, K4C, *K8A, K4C, rep from * to last 7[8:9] sts, K7[8:9]A.

4th row P7(8:9)A, *P1A, P2C, P9A, rep from * ending last rep P8[9:10]A.

Cont in st st in A only until hat measures 22[23:25]cm from beg, ending with a WS row.

Next row K0[2:1], *K3 tog, rep from * to end.

Thread yarn through rem sts, pull tightly and fasten off securely.

Finishing the hat

Sew the back hat seam. Make a pompon and sew it on top of the hat. To make the pompon, cut two card discs equal in diameter to the required size of the pompon (approximately 8cm). Cut smaller circles from the centre of each. Using colour A, wind the yarn closely around both discs, placed together, passing it through the centre and back over the outer edge each time, until the central hole is filled in.

With sharp scissors, cut through all the layers of yarn at the edges of the discs. Wind a length of yarn several times around the centre of the pompon, between the two discs, and knot tightly.

Cut away the card and fluff out the pompon. If necessary, trim away any projecting ends, and use the tying ends to attach the pompon to the hat.

Sew the berries in position as illustrated.

Right mitten

Using smaller needles and A, cast on 37[39:41] sts. Work in K1, P1, rib for 4cm, inc 1 st in last row. 38[40:42] sts. Change to larger needles and beg with a K row, work 2 rows in st st.

Shape thumb gusset
Beg snowflake on palm as foll:
1st row K18[19:20]A, M1, K2A, M1, K8[9:9]A, K2C, K8[8:9].
2nd row P7[7:8]A, P4C, P29[31:32]A.
3rd row K18[19:20]A, M1, K4A, M1, K7[8:8]A, K4C, K7[7:8]A.
4th row P8[8:9]A, P2C, P32[34:35]A.
Beg holly on back of hand as foll:
1st row K7A, K8B, K3[4:5]A, M1, K6A, M1, K18[19:20]A.
2nd row P29[31:33]A, P8B, K7A.
These 2 rows set the holly patt, cont to work holly from chart on back of mitten, keeping palm in A only and inc as before until there are 52[54:56] sts.
Next row K1A, K2B, K2A, K6B, K23[24:25]A turn.
Next row P16[16:18]A, turn. Work across these stitches for the thumb. Work 3[4:4]cm in st st on these 16[16:16]sts ending with a WS row.

Shape top of thumb

Next row K2 tog to end of row. 8[8:8]

sts.
P one row.
Cut yarn, thread through rem sts, pull tightly and fasten off.
With RS facing rejoin yarn to base of thumb, K up 2 sts from base of thumb and K18[19:20]sts to end. 38[40:42] sts
P one row, keeping holly patt correct.
Beg working snowflake patt on palm as foll:
Next row K1A, K6B, K17[18:19]A, K2C, K12[13:14]A.
Next row P11[12:13]A, P4C, P16[17:18]A, P6B, P1A.
Next row K23[24:25]A, K4C, K11[12:13]A.
Next row P12[13:14]A, P2C, P24[25:26]A.
Work 12 rows in st st using A only.
Beg working snowflake patt as foll:
Next row K6[7:8]A, *K2C, K10A, rep from * once, K2C, K6[7:8]A.
Next row P5[6:7]A, *P4C, P8A, rep from * once, P4C, P5[6:7]A.
Next row K5[6:7]A, *K4C, K8A, rep from * once, K4C, K5[6:7]A.
Next row P6[7:8]A, *P2C, P10A, rep from * once, P2C, P6[7:8]A.
Using A only cont in st st until mitten measures 7[8:9]cm from base of thumb, ending with a WS row.

Shape top of mitten

1st row *K1, K2 tog, K13[14:15], K2 tog tbl, K1, rep from * to end.
2nd and every alt row P to end.
3rd row *K1, K2 tog, K11[12:13], K2 tog tbl, K1, rep from * to end.
5th row *K1, K2 tog, K9[10:11], K2 tog tbl, K1, rep from * to end.
7th row *K1, K2 tog, K7[8:9], K2 tog tbl, K1, rep from * to end.
8th row P.
Cast off.

Left mitten

As right mitten reversing position of patt.

Finishing the mittens

Sew the thumb, top and side seams on each mitten. Sew the berries in position.

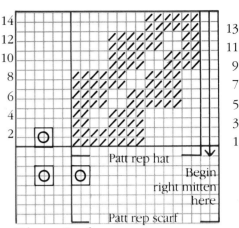

Patt rep hat

Begin right mitten here

Patt rep scarf

Edge sts Scarf

Key

A

B

Approx position for sewing on bead

Materials

Apron

3m of 90cm-wide plain, unbleached calico

4m of 12.5-wide broderie anglaise trim

1.5m of 2.5-wide pre-gathered broderie anglaise trim

10cm of self-adhesive fastening

Matching sewing thread

Tailor's chalk or coloured pencil

Tracing paper and long ruler

Gloves

40cm of 90cm-wide cream, pre-quilted fabric

20cm of 90cm-wide plain, unbleached calico

1.1m of cream bias binding

Matching sewing thread

Motifs

Tracing paper

Transfer pencil

Red and white fabric paints

Black permanent marker pen

Paintbrush

Cook's Christmas

Christmas can be a nerve-wracking time for the cook – at least until guests are eating and the compliments start coming in – so this pretty, old-fashioned calico apron, with its heart-shaped pockets and lacy trim, together with matching oven gloves, all cheerfully featuring Father Christmas himself, will be a welcome morale booster.

The set is so pretty and easily laundered that it could equally well be made without the Christmas motif, though the idea of having an apron reserved for the festive season has a charm of its own. On the practical side, it provides a perfect solution to the familiar problem of having to appear attractively dressed without risking damage to an expensive outfit.

Note Make sure when you buy the paints and the fabric that they are compatible: some transfer colours can only be used with synthetic fabrics and most fabric paints can only be used with natural fibres such as cotton, so check carefully and if you are not using calico for the apron and gloves, make sure that you know the constituency of the fabric that you have chosen.

Cutting out

The first stage is to cut out the pattern pieces before transferring the design. For the apron, mark the pattern pieces on the fabric using a long ruler and either tailor's chalk or a coloured pencil.

All the pattern pieces are cut out on the straight grain of the fabric. For the pockets, trace off the shape given on page 138, and cut out. When cutting out the fabric place the pattern to a fold as instructed – it is easier to match the two sides of the heart if you cut out the pockets on the fold in this way. If you are also making the gloves, trace off the glove pattern given on pages 142-143.

For the apron, cut out the pattern pieces as follows:

Front – 90cm wide x 80cm deep, cut one

Sides – 32cm wide x 80cm deep, cut two

Waistband – 60cm wide x 8cm deep, cut two

Straps – 8cm wide x 90cm long, cut four

Tie ends – 15cm wide x 90cm long, cut two

Bib – 20cm wide x 26cm deep, cut two

Pocket – heart shape, cut four

For the gloves, cut out three matching pairs from quilted fabric.

If the calico to be used for the apron and the tops of the oven gloves has had any finishing chemical added to it, this might prevent the transfer design from colouring the fabric effectively, so wash the bib section and the non-quilted glove fabric and press them with a moderately hot iron. Mark the outlines of a matching pair of gloves on the plain calico.

Transferring the design

Trace over the design, using the transfer pencil. Do not trace the central registration mark with the transfer pencil, but copy this on the other side of the tracing, using an ordinary pencil.

Fold and press the bib section diagonally in half both ways and press, to find the centre point. Lay the bib flat on your ironing board or pressing table and either pin it or put strips of masking tape at the corners to hold it in position. Matching the central registration mark on the tracing with the pressed centre of the bib, carefully place the design, transfer side down, over the fabric and, using a moderately hot iron, press until the outlines appear on the calico.

For the gloves, you will need to make two separate tracings of the motif in order to reverse one motif to give a mirror image: make one tracing using the transfer pencil and for the

Cutting layout

Fold

Selvedges

Front

Waistband

Side panels

Strap

Strap

Strap

Strap

Tie end

Tie end

Bib

Pocket

Bib

Pocket

second one trace the motif with an
ordinary pencil and then turn it over
and trace over the outlines on the
back of the tracing, this time using the
transfer pencil. Ignore the registration
marks but carefully place the tracings
over the fabric with the marked
outlines, fitting them within the same

space in each outline. Again using a
moderately hot iron to make, press
two matching Father Christmases.

Go over the details on the bib and
the gloves, this time using the black
permanent marker pen. As when
ironing, it will be easier if you tape or
pin the fabric to your working surface.

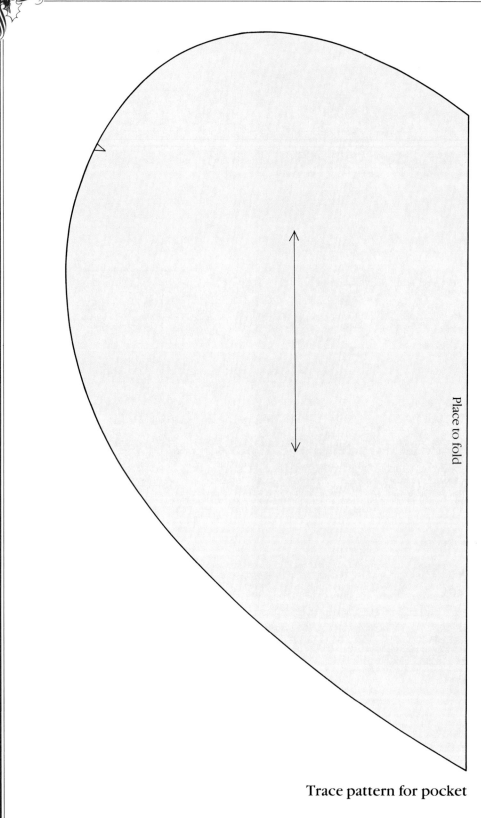

Place to fold

Trace pattern for pocket

Using the paintbrush, paint the red details on all three Father Christmases, then paint the white details, taking care not to go over the marked lines.

Permanently fix the fabric paint to the fabric by ironing, following the manufacturer's instructions.

Alternative method

If, instead of using calico or other natural fibre for the apron and glove tops, you have chosen a synthetic fabric, and if you are using transfer crayons instead of paints, the design is transferred by a slightly different process. Start by transferring the design to the fabric and going over the lines with the permanent marker, as already described.

When the outlines are on the fabric, take the tracings and, using red and white crayons, colour in the details of the design on the three tracings. If the crayons do not work well on the tracing paper, you will have to copy the design on cartridge paper (again, three times, with one matching pair of heads) and colour this. Take care not to leave any loose flakes of crayon on the coloured drawings as these may mark the wrong part of the fabric. Cut the drawings out, cutting carefully around the outlines, again to avoid smudges.

Carefully place the coloured drawings face down on the fabric and press, first making sure that your iron is not too hot for the fabric.

The apron
Preparing the skirt

With right sides together and taking a 1.5cm seam allowance, stitch the side sections to the front panel. Press open and neaten.

At each side of the combined panel, turn under the raw edge for 1cm and press, then turn under a further 1.5cm and press, then straight stitch, close to the folded edge, to neaten the sides.

Run two lines of gathering threads along the upper edge of the apron, starting 5cm in from each end.

Pockets

Take one pocket piece (this now becomes a top pocket piece) and pin pre-gathered broderie anglaise trim all around, matching the raw edge of the pocket with the raw, gathered edge of the trim, so that the lace lies on the right side of the pocket. Allow fullness around the curves. Pin and stitch the trim in position, taking a scant 1cm seam.

Place a second pocket piece (now pocket lining) on the first, with right sides together, and machine stitch around, leaving a 4cm opening at one side for turning and taking a 1cm seam allowance (take care that the first stitching line will not show when the pocket is turned out). Trim the seam and clip the curves, then turn the pocket right side out. Slipstitch the opening.

Repeat the process to prepare the second pocket. Pin the pockets to the skirt front with the outer notch 36cm in from the side seam and 16.5cm down from the raw upper edge. Make sure the pockets are evenly positioned and then topstitch to secure, stitching around the lower edge, between the notches.

Bib

With right sides together stitch the painted bib front to the bib lining along the upper edge, taking a 1.5cm seam. Trim, turn and press the seam. Baste the lower edges together. Fold the bib to find the centre of the lower edge and put a marker there.

Straps

The four strap pieces represent two top pieces and two lining pieces. Cut the remaining broderie anglaise trim in half. Taper the ends of each lace strip as shown. Run a gathering thread along the raw edge of each strip.

Take one strap piece and pull up the gathers on a lace strip to fit the strap, starting and finishing 3.5cm from the short edges. Pin and stitch the lace to the strap, with right sides

Trace pattern for Father Christmas motif

Centre

together and raw edges matching. Press the seam towards the strap and trim it to 6mm. Repeat for the other strap.

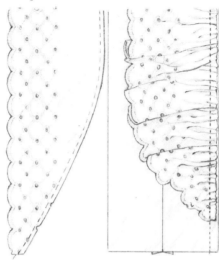

With right sides together and raw edges matching, pin and baste the straps to the outside edges of the bib.

On each strap lining, turn under a 1.5cm allowance along one long edge and press, then trim the allowance to 6mm. Pin the strap linings (unpressed long edges) to the back of the bib, so the bib is sandwiched between the strap fronts and linings. Also pin the free ends of the straps and linings together, continuing on from the bib. Stitch the long edge of the straps, on the inside of the bib and across the short end. Trim the seam and cut across the corner. Press the seams flat and turn the strap pieces to the right side, then pin and tack the folded edge of the linings to the fronts and topstitch working from the right side.

Finishing the apron
Pull up the skirt gathers to fit the waistband, starting and finishing 1.5cm from either end of the band. Pin and stitch, then press the seam allowances towards the band.

At each side of the skirt and band, turn back the ungathered 5cm to form a self facing and press. Baste in position at the waistband.

Fold the skirt to find the centre of the waistband and mark.

Take one of the tie pieces and make a 5mm double hem on both long sides. Fold the tie with right sides together and machine stitch taking a 5mm allowance, across one short end. Turn right side out forming the end into a point, and press flat. Pleat the

other end of the tie to fit the depth of the waistband, with the finished edge of the tie 1.5cm below the raw top edge of the waistband. Stitch the tie to the waistband.

Repeat for the second tie, and attach it in the same way.

With right sides and centre fronts matching, pin and baste the bib to the waistband. On the remaining waistband facing, press one long (lower) edge 1.5cm to the wrong side. Place the waistband facing wrong side uppermost over the bib, matching the raw edge of the waistband. Pin and baste in position along the top edge of the waistband and the short sides, making sure that the ties lie inwards, between the two bands. Stitch along the top edge and down both sides. Stitch across the ties and bib section a second time for added strength.

Trim seams and cut across the seam allowances at the corners, then turn right side out and slipstitch the folded edge of the waistband facing to the previous row of stitching.

Oven glove
Cut out the decorated glove fronts along the marked outline.

With wrong sides together, stitch one decorated front to one quilted glove piece, taking a 1cm seam. Repeat for the other glove, then stitch

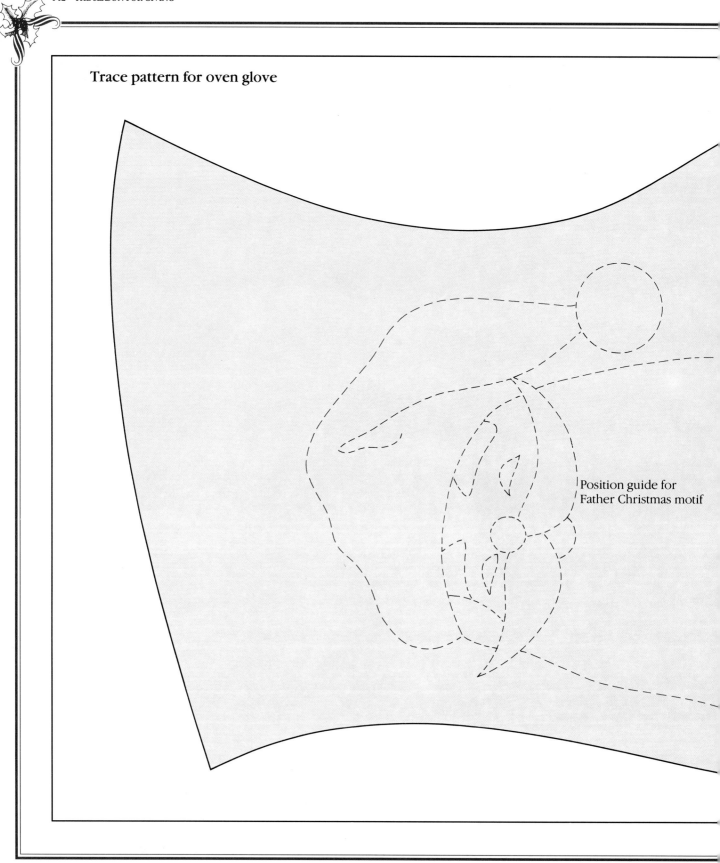

Trace pattern for oven glove

Position guide for
Father Christmas motif

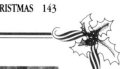

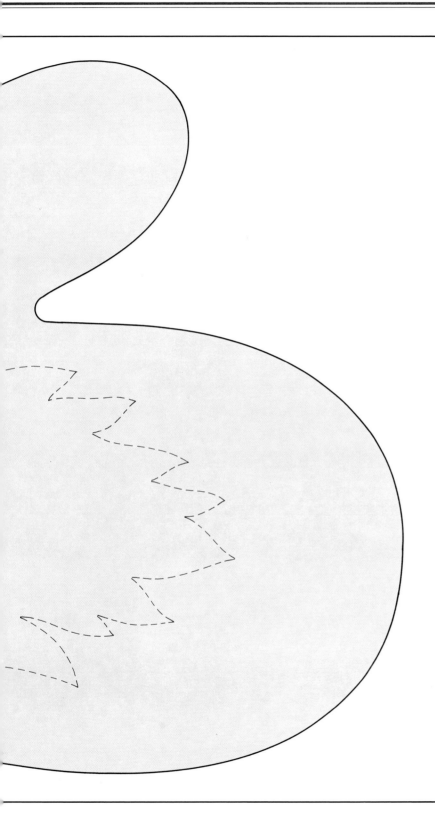

the two pairs of quilted glove pieces together, this time with wrong sides together.

At the seam allowances of the quilted fabric, unpick the quilting to the seamline and trim back the wadding as close to the stitching as possible, to remove excess bulk. Trim the seam allowances of the fabric and clip the curves at the thumb.

Turn decorated glove sections right side out and insert a quilted glove inside each one.

On each glove, trim the inner lining at the wrist edge, to within 9mm from the wrist edge of the outer glove. Catchstitch in position at the seams and to the inside layer of fabric at the back of the outer glove.

Machine stitch bias binding to the wrist edge of each glove, stitching it to the right side and taking a 6mm seam allowance. Fold the binding to the wrong side so that it is not visible on the right side, and slipstitch in place. For each glove, cut a 17cm strip from the remaining binding and fold it in half lengthways, with right sides together. Stitch close to the folded edges, then fold the strip into a loop and stitch it to the side seam of the glove, on the inside.

Materials
One or more wooden spoons
Pyrograph machine or wood-burning
    tool (both are electrically heated)
Fine glasspaper
Trace-down paper (available from artist's
    suppliers) – optional
Water-colours, poster paints or blendable
    colour pencils
A firm, fine paintbrush
Varnish (an aerosol spray is the
    easiest to use)
30cm each of red, green and white
    1cm-wide satin ribbon

For the cook

These wooden spoons have been
festively decorated using a technique
called pyrography, a craft which has
been practised throughout the ages
and throughout the world. The design
outlines are lightly burned onto a
wooden surface, producing a slightly
raised appearance, which may be
lesser or greater according to the
degree of burning.

A simple wood-burning tool is not
expensive to buy and can be obtained
from an arts and crafts supplier. If you
do not want to try out this craft, you
can obtain a similar effect by drawing
the motifs on the spoons with a
drawing pen.

Wooden spoons are available in
kitchen and hardware shops. It is best
to choose spoons made of smooth
wood of a light colour and with an
even grain, as these will show the
motifs and colours to the best
advantage.

Burning the design

Using a piece of fine glasspaper, thoroughly sand down the spoon, working in the direction of the grain until a smooth surface is obtained.

Either pencil in the motif of your choice, or make a tracing from the motifs given and copy it to the back of the spoon with trace-down paper (any mistakes will be easier to rub away than those made by ordinary carbon paper). Keep the lines clear and distinct, and make them as lightly as possible.

If a pyrograph tool is being used, always work on a heatproof surface and away from young children. Attach a medium to fine point (this is equivalent to the nib of a pen) and heat the point until it is just short of red hot. Test it on a spare piece of wood to make sure that it does not burn too fast or too fiercely.

Any lines which are over-burned cannot be lessened, so it is best to work the design as lightly as possible, if necessary going over lines that are too faint a second time. Make the outline first, then the inner lines and details. Burn spots will appear if the point stops even for a second, so keep it moving. Once the pyrography is completed, gently rub out any remaining pencil marks with a clean, white rubber.

Alternative method

If the motif is to be drawn with a pen instead of burned into the wood, the wood should be sealed after sanding with a sanding sealer solution, obtainable from hardware shops. This will prevent the ink from bleeding into the grain of the wood.

Experiment on a spare piece of wood to make sure that your pen is suitable before drawing the outline on the spoon.

Colouring and finishing

To colour in the motifs, use sharpened, blendable colour pencils, or apply water-colours or poster paints with a small, firm paintbrush. Keep within the marked outlines.

Allow the decorations to dry thoroughly, preferably overnight, and then give the spoon several light coats of spray varnish until you have obtained a suitable finish.

Complete each spoon with a satin bow, tied round the handle.

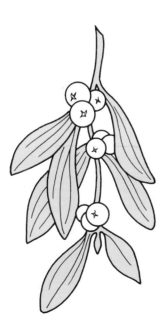
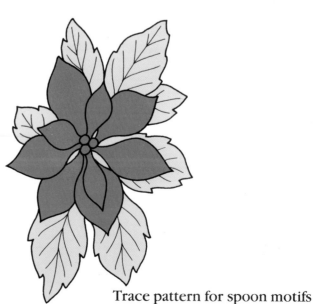

Trace pattern for spoon motifs

Quantities

This is sufficient for two Father
Christmases (complete with sleigh) and
six kings.

300g plain flour
100g margarine
125g golden syrup
50g caster sugar
3 teaspoons fresh root ginger (grated on
   the fine side of a cheese grater)
1 teaspoon bicarbonate of soda
1 teaspoon ground cinnamon
1 egg

Decoration

225g icing sugar
Jelly diamonds
Icing balls (in mixed colours)
Sugar strands
Hundreds and thousands
Green, red, blue and yellow food
   colouring

Templates

Tracing paper
Medium-weight card
Spray glue
Scalpel

Gingernut figures

These gingernut kings and Father
Christmas (pulling his own sleigh to
give the reindeer a rest) are so
decorative that it will be hard to start
eating them, and so delicious that it
will be hard to stop once you break
through your inhibitions. Children
will love helping to make them and
adding the finishing touches. In fact if
you are giving a small children's party
it would be fun to prepare the dough
and the templates beforehand, make
the biscuits together at the party, and
let each child take one home as a
parting gift.

Making templates

First trace the outlines of the kings
and Father Christmas. Cut out the
shapes, leaving a margin of about 1cm
around each one.

   Using spray glue, attach the tracing
paper outlines to card, then cut out,
following the outlines accurately.

Making the biscuits

Measure the syrup into a cup and
stand it in a pan of hot water to warm,
or microwave it for a few seconds.

   Heat the oven to 150°C/300°F/Gas 2
and grease two baking sheets.

   Mix the fat and sugar and then add
the dry ingredients, the well-beaten
egg and the syrup. Mix until you have
a stiff dough. Knead the dough very
thoroughly.

   Roll the dough out on a floured
board until it is about 1cm deep. Place
the templates in position. Using either
a very sharp kitchen knife or the
scalpel, cut around the outlines.

   Carefully tidy any rough edges with
your fingers then, using a slice, gently
lift the shapes and arrange them on
the baking sheets. Make sure that you
allow plenty of space around each
biscuit.

   Bake for one hour (for softer
biscuits, bake for 10 to 15 minutes at
180°C/350°F/Gas 4, though these may
not hold their shape quite so well).

   After baking, place the biscuits on a
wire rack to cool.

Decorating the biscuits

Make glacé icing: sift the icing sugar
into a bowl and then beat in enough
water to give a thick consistency
suitable for piping.

   Divide the icing into five cups and
add drops of food colouring, mixing it
in until you have one cup with the
original white icing, one cup with red,
one with green, one blue and one
with yellow (add a very small quantity
of red if necessary, to achieve a gold
colour). You will only require a small
quantity of the gold, and more red and
white than blue and green.

   Using a wide nozzle, pipe the icing
onto the biscuits. Cover all the areas in
any one colour and allow it to dry
before changing to the next.

   When you have finished icing, add
the cake decorations as indicated on
the diagrams. They must all be added
immediately you have finished icing,
before the icing has hardened.

   The finished biscuits can be stored
for up to three weeks in an airtight tin.

Trace patterns for gingernut figures

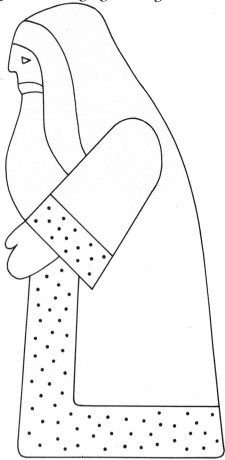

Father Christmas and sleigh

Three kings

CHAPTER 6

The Christmas table

Every skilled hostess knows that it is not just excellent and beautifully presented food, but those all-important finishing touches that create a certain atmosphere and turn a delicious meal into a special and memorable occasion. The right lighting, such as a set of the angel candleholders featured here, an attractive centrepiece, special mats and napkins, made just for the day, and perhaps the jolly Father Christmas rings shown on page 158 – they are all part of the Christmas scene, and help to transform a familiar room into a magical setting that will stay in the mind of every child present for a lifetime.

Materials

2m of 90cm-wide heavy white cotton drill or similar fabric (this is sufficient for six mats and a runner for a 1.9m-long table)

Sylko sewing thread (50) in green 046 (for the zigzag outlining)

Anchor stranded embroidery thread: one skein of red 305 (for the berries)

Dressmaker's carbon paper

Tracing paper

Paper (A3 size, for making pattern – see below)

Ruler and pencil

Sharp embroidery scissors

Embroidery hoop, 20cm across (optional)

Holly mats

A beautiful table setting, with embroidered mats and runner, creates a festive atmosphere, emphasizing that this is a special occasion. The mats shown here are embroidered largely by machine so they are relatively quick to make, and though you may use them for Christmas parties and for the twelve days of Christmas itself, they can be taken out each year to mark the start of the season. The mats shown here are plain white, but the background could equally well be pale green or yellow if either of those would complement your china.

Making the pattern

For the placemat, first trace off the semi-circle, given on page 154, tracing the outline in parallel lines, as shown, and reversing it on the centre line, to complete the oval mat. On the same tracing, trace off the holly motif in a similar way, positioning it at one corner, as indicated by dashed lines.

The pattern for the runner is made in a similar way, with a straight strip of paper 26cm wide and a semi-circle at each end. An overall length of 1m would be appropriate for a 1.9m table, assuming that there would be a place setting at each end of the table, but the best way to be sure that you have got the length of the runner right is to measure your own dining table before making the pattern.

Alternatively, you may prefer a longer runner (allowing the ends to fall over the edges of the table), with place settings along each long side.

Embroidery

Using dressmaker's carbon paper, transfer the outlines of the mats and the runner on the fabric, using the paper patterns and positioning the shapes as shown in the cutting layout. Remember that the holly motif projects beyond the oval outline and allow extra space between mats.

Set your sewing machine to a close zigzag and stitch around the edges of the mats and the outlines of the holly leaves. You will probably find it easier to do this if you first cut the mats apart, but leave a margin of spare fabric at least 3cm wide around each mat, including the motifs. If you cut too close to the outline, the stitching will not be so easy to work.

Some people find it easier to work machine satin stitch (close zigzag) if the fabric is held in an embroidery hoop. In this case, do not cut out the mats, but put the fabric in a small hoop so that the holly motif is in the centre of the ring and the fabric can lie flat on the machine, marked side up. This will save you having to hold

Cutting layout

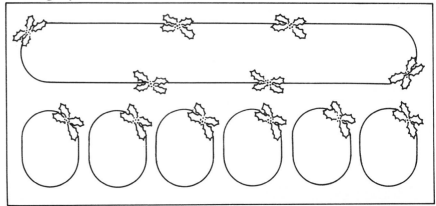

Place to fold

Trace pattern for mat

Position guide for holly motif

the fabric taut as you stitch the details of the motifs. The outlines of the mats can more easily be worked without a hoop.

The berries are hand embroidered in straight satin stitch, using three strands of embroidery thread. To work the satin stitch, bring the needle up on one edge of the berry, carry the thread across to the opposite edge and return under the fabric close to the starting point. Work the next stitch close to the first, making sure that no background fabric shows in between. For a raised effect, work over the stitches a second time, so that the

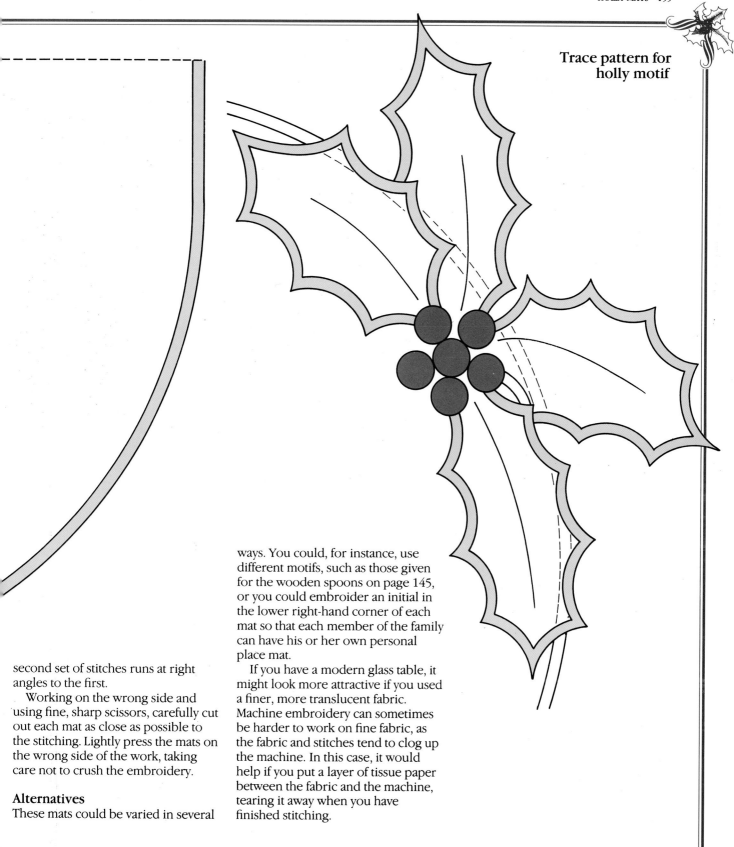

**Trace pattern for
holly motif**

ways. You could, for instance, use different motifs, such as those given for the wooden spoons on page 145, or you could embroider an initial in the lower right-hand corner of each mat so that each member of the family can have his or her own personal place mat.

If you have a modern glass table, it might look more attractive if you used a finer, more translucent fabric. Machine embroidery can sometimes be harder to work on fine fabric, as the fabric and stitches tend to clog up the machine. In this case, it would help if you put a layer of tissue paper between the fabric and the machine, tearing it away when you have finished stitching.

second set of stitches runs at right angles to the first.

Working on the wrong side and using fine, sharp scissors, carefully cut out each mat as close as possible to the stitching. Lightly press the mats on the wrong side of the work, taking care not to crush the embroidery.

Alternatives
These mats could be varied in several

Materials
Red napkin
Two small jingle bells
1.2m of 3mm-wide emerald green ribbon
Fabric glue
Short length of fine wire
White napkin
27 large green leaf sequins
Eight 3mm-diameter red plastic beads
Three 5mm-diameter red plastic beads
White sewing thread
Green napkin
Oddments of lace trim
Bonding web or fabric glue

Christmas napkins

Small finishing touches like these decorated napkins, with their added trims, make all the difference to a Christmas table setting. Purchased napkins have been used here, but you could easily make your own by hemming 40cm squares of an appropriate fabric. Vary the colours of the ribbon and the sequins and use different lace motifs so that each guest has his or her own individual pattern.

Red napkin
Cut two pieces of ribbon 20cm long and two pieces each 11.5cm long. Thread a 20cm length into a long-eyed needle and leaving an end about 2cm long on the under-side of the napkin, stitch up to a corner, starting 15.5cm in from the corner 1.5cm from the edge. Sew with long running stitches, about 1cm in length, and stop 1.5cm from each edge, at the corner. Secure the other end to the under-side with a spot of fabric glue and leave a tail of ribbon at the corner.

Thread the remaining 20cm length of ribbon and starting from the opposite side, sew up to the same corner. Tie the two ends of ribbon into a neat knot, then thread a jingle bell on each tail and knot them on.

Using fabric glue, glue the two 11.5cm strips to the napkin to meet in a corner, keeping parallel to the first two pieces and 3cm in from the edge of the napkin.

Set aside an 8cm piece of the remaining length of ribbon and wind the rest around a 5cm-wide piece of card. Slide the ribbon off the card and secure the loops together at the centre by wrapping the fine wire around them. Push the ends of the wire through the knots securing the jingle bells. Use the remaining piece of ribbon to cover the wire join and leave two ends coming down between the bells like the two ends of an ordinary bow.

Spread out the four ribbon ends

which now hang down from the bells so that two ends lie to one side of the corner and two to the other. Use small dots of glue to secure the ends in this pattern, completing the napkin.

White napkin
Measure 2.5cm up from the edge of the napkin and 11.5cm from the edge at one corner. Place the tip of a leaf sequin at this point and sew it in position. Attach a small red bead to the base of the leaf then sew two more leaves at an angle to the first, with their bases approximately 5mm from that of the first, making a small cluster.

Repeat the process to make three more clusters, always working towards the corner and keeping parallel to the edge of the napkin.

Measure away from the corner again and repeat the process on the other side of the corner, making four more clusters. Fill the space that remains at the corner with the last three sequins and the three larger beads.

Green napkin
At one corner of the napkin, make a pattern with the lace motifs, cutting them apart first if necessary. When you are happy with the arrangement, fuse the motifs to the napkin using bonding web.

Father Christmas napkin ring

A delightful piece of fun to complete your table setting, these frivolous napkin rings are very quick to make and guarantee that your Christmas dinner will start with laughter. The ring itself is just the hair and the face: the body is formed from a folded paper napkin. The quantities given below are sufficient for one ring only, but when you are making rings ready for the day, make a few more than the anticipated number of your guests in case there are any last-minute additions to the party.

Method

Trace off the outline and make a template (see page 50). Use the template to draw the outline on the back of the fur fabric, making sure that the fur will run down from the top of the finished ring. Cut out the shape, then mark and cut out the central face shape. The face fabric must be carefully cut in one piece and kept, to be used for the whiskers.

Glue the felt rectangle to the wrong side over the cut out face area. Brush the fur carefully in position around the face and trim it above the face. Glue the eyes in position.

Fold the cut-out fur section in half lengthways and glue the wrong sides together. Form the strands into whiskers and glue the additional whiskers to the bottom of the face. Attach the berries to the holly and glue the decoration in position to one side of the face.

Trim away the fur for 1.5cm at one end of the piece and glue the other end over this to form a ring.

Materials

Approximately 20cm x 10cm of white fur fabric with a long, silky pile
4cm x 4.5cm of flesh-coloured felt
Two 5mm-diameter eyes with movable centres
Small, three-leaf paper holly triangle
Two red berries
Fabric glue
Red paper table napkin
Tracing paper and lightweight card

Trace pattern for beard

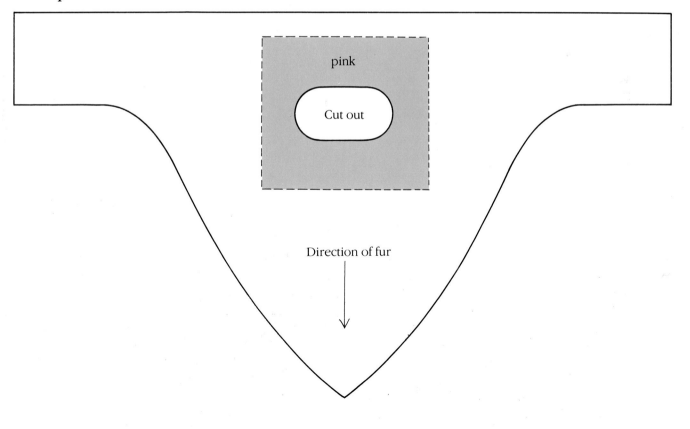

Materials

25cm polystyrene ring filled with
    absorbent foam (available from
    florists)
Sprigs of cypress, pine, holly and ivy
20 small pine cones
30 holly berries (available from florists
    – if your holly has no berries)
Gold spray
1.2m of 2.5cm-wide red ribbon
Stub wire (available from florists)
Four medium-sized red candles

Evergreen centrepiece

Candlelight adds softness and a
glowing lustre to a Christmas table set
with gleaming silver and crystal,
creating the right ambience for a
memorable occasion. This evergreen
circle, set with four candles, is very
quick and easy to make and can be
prepared in advance (though not so
far ahead that the greenery looks tired
on the day). Take care that you do not
leave the room unattended while the
candles are lit, in case they burn too
far down. Any drips of wax should be
caught in the greenery, but you might
want to put a mat or a circle of foil
underneath the centrepiece.

Preparation

Spray the pine cones and let them dry
on a sheet of newspaper before wiring
them with 20cm lengths of stub wire
(see page 12).

   Gather the holly berries into
bunches of twos and threes and bind
them together with lengths of florist's
stub wire.

   Cut the ribbon into four equal
lengths and tie each length into a bow.
Thread a length of stub wire through
the back of the knot of each bow.

   Thoroughly soak the oasis until it
has absorbed as much water as
possible.

Making the centrepiece

Work on a flat surface, turning the ring
around as you work and constantly
checking to make sure that you have
an even distribution. It will help if you
first arrange the greenery into
bunches, according to kind.

   Start at the outer edge of the circle,
alternating sprigs of cypress and holly
and pushing them firmly into the ring.
Make sure that the circle does not
become misshapen.

   At the top of the ring, push in the
ivy, pine cones, berries and ribbons,
arranging the cones in circles where
you intend to position the candles. Fill
the inner edge of the circle with small
sprigs of pine.

   Finish by pushing the candles firmly
into the ring. Incidentally, if you are
unfortunate enough to end up with a
few drops of candle wax on your
tablecloth, the best way to remove
them is by pressing the cloth between
layers of absorbent paper, using a
reasonably hot iron.

Angel candle holder

Made from wood and decorated with acrylic paints, this little angel is designed to shed gentle candlelight on your Christmas festivities. The wood quantities given are sufficient for just one angel, which would look charming as a centrepiece inside a table decoration. If you are feeling ambitious, you could make several, to face out from the centre of the table. The design is carefully contrived so that the wings counterbalance the front portion, which holds a small size Christmas candle. Do not use long candles or you will spoil the look of the design and, more importantly, make it unstable.

Cutting the pieces

You do not need a special carpentry bench for this simple piece, but when cutting the wood always secure it to the table edge with a clamp. Protect the table and the wood surface with either folded up newspaper or flat wood offcuts. Do not attempt to cut unsecured wood.

For best results, use good quality acrylic paint and matt varnish. In the same way, check the wood carefully before you buy it and reject any pieces that have knots or may have been split. If you do have to use wood with knots in, seal these with knotting varnish before painting.

First trace the pattern for the body and transfer it to the 20mm thick wood. It is essential to make absolutely sure that the line at the base of the foot is straight, as the overall balance of the candle holder depends on this. Secure the marked wood to a table with a strong clamp and then cut the base line and any other reasonably straight lines with a hacksaw. Use a fretsaw for the finer curves.

Cut the 10mm thick wood in half and bind the two pieces firmly together with masking tape. Trace the wing and arm patterns and transfer

these to the wood following the straight grain. Using a combination of hacksaw and fretsaw as before, cut through the doubled wood to cut a pair of wings and a pair of arms. Once again, make sure before you start that the wood is secured to the table top with a strong clamp.

Trace and transfer the flower-shaped candle base to a remaining piece of the 10mm thick wood. A hole will be drilled at the centre of the shape for the candle, so before you start, secure the wood to the table with a clamp, placing a scrap piece of wood underneath the area to be drilled. This will help to avoid splitting.

Using the brace and bit, drill a hole in the centre of the flower shape, drilling right through the wood, then carefully cut around the flower outline with a fretsaw.

Mark out the rectangular shape, which is combined with the flower to make the holder, on a scrap of 20mm thick wood. Cut it out carefully, making sure that you have a perfect cube, with the cut sides absolutely at right angles to the top and bottom. In the finished holder, the cube is turned on edge and the candle is held in one long (cut) side edge of this cube.

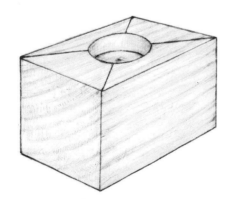

When you have cut the cube, therefore, turn it so that this side faces up. Lightly pencil in diagonal lines from corner to corner across this side to find the centre point, then drill the centre to a depth of 5mm, using the same bit as before.

Materials

23cm x 10cm of 20mm thick deal (planed and ready for use)
50cm x 10cm of 10mm deal (planed and ready for use)
One 3cm panel pin
Woodworking adhesive
White and gold acrylic paint
Matt varnish
One large and one fine sable brush for painting the details in acrylic paint
Brush for varnish

Tools

Hacksaw
Fretsaw
Brace and 15mm drill bit
Clamps
Medium and fine sandpaper
Flat and curved sanding blocks

Mark the centre of the base of the cube and gently tap the panel pin into place. This sticks into the base of the candle to hold it secure.

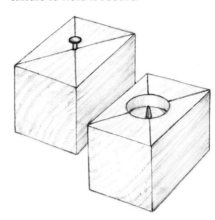

Sand the cube and the candle base, sanding the rims as well as the surfaces and using a combination of the flat and rounded sanding blocks. Start with the medium sandpaper and finish with the fine. Where possible, sand along the grain of the wood.

Sand the arms and the wings in the same way, making sure that the palms of the hands are flat. Sand the body of the angel, checking carefully that the feet are level and will stand firmly on a flat surface.

Painting and assembly

Using the larger sable brush and white paint, paint the cube and the dress, covering both sides of the body and stopping at the neck. Paint the arms white to the wrist, leaving the hand and the inside surface of each arm unpainted. Leave them to dry.

Paint the hair, wings and feet and the side and top edges of the flower-shaped candle base with gold paint. Leave them to dry.

When the body is completely dry, use the fine brush and the gold paint to make the decorative lines and dots of gold on the dress. If necessary, paint these details twice.

The final stage is to glue the pieces together. Use a good quality woodworking adhesive and at each

stage allow the glue to dry thoroughly before moving on to the next. Start by gluing the flower-shaped candle base to the cube, matching up the drill holes. Leave it to dry.

Next glue the hands to the cube: place the hands parallel to and just under the base of the candle base. Use a scrap piece of 20mm-thick wood as a spacer at the shoulder end to keep the arms a parallel distance apart. When

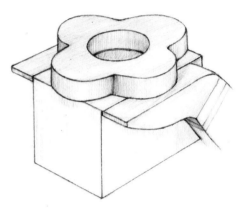

the hands are firmly attached to the holder and the glue has dried, glue the arms to the body, following the lines marked on the pattern.

The position of the wings is crucial to the balance of the body, so mark the gluing line carefully on each side of the body. Double-check by attaching the wings to the body with masking tape and mark the correct position carefully.

Glue the wings to the body. As with the arms, use a scrap piece of 20mm-thick wood as a spacer to hold the wings absolutely parallel to each other while the glue dries.

Leave the assembled angel for 12 hours and then give it a coating of matt varnish. Leave it to dry and then apply a second coat.

Warning

As the candle holder is made of wood it will ignite if the candle is left to burn away, so never leave it unattended!

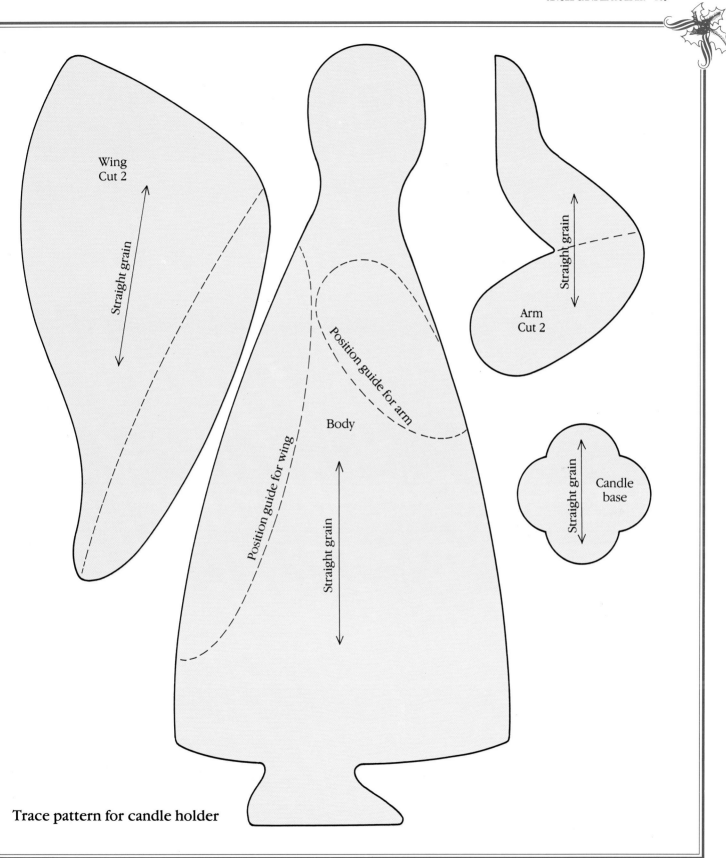

Wing
Cut 2

Straight grain

Position guide for arm

Body

Position guide for wing

Straight grain

Arm
Cut 2

Straight grain

Straight grain

Candle
base

Trace pattern for candle holder

Index

Acknowledgements

Project contributors
Jeanette Appleton: page 80
Gisella Banbury: pages 42, 124
Sheila Coulson: page 152
Alan Dart: page 113
Caroline Dewing: pages 32, 118
Julia Dumbrell: page 132
Valerie Green: page 115
David Hawcock: pages 27, 36, 39, 67, 74, 77, 95
Christina Korth: pages 12, 23, 160
Shelley Lazar: page 84
Fiona Neville: page 163
Bonnie Phipps: pages 50, 91, 146
Fiona Ryan: pages 21, 144
Pamela Westland: pages 15, 16, 18
Gloria Wittke: pages 44, 47, 54, 58, 88, 128, 136, 156, 159

Illustrators
Denis Hawkins: page 131(br)
Sally Holmes: pages 12, 15, 20, 22, 25, 26, 28, 32, 34, 37, 39, 41, 43, 44, 77, 92(t), 116, 120, 126, 128, 129(b), 140, 146, 156, 163, 164
John Hutchinson: pages 23, 28(t), 29, 35, 36, 40, 42, 46, 49, 52/3, 54, 55/6, 61, 62/3, 68/9, 70/1, 72/3, 74, 78/9, 82/3, 86, 88/9, 92(b), 93, 98/9, 100/1, 102/3, 117, 118, 121, 126(bl), 127, 129(t), 135, 137, 138/9, 142, 145, 148/9, 152, 154/5, 159, 165
Coral Mula: page 131(c)

Photographers
Simon Butcher: pages 106, 108, 110, 111, 112
Christmas Archives & Photo Library: pages 7, 8, 10, 16, 30, 64, 104, 122, 143, 148, 150, 160
Ray Duns: pages 13(r), 14, 15, 17, 18/19, 21, 27, 32/3, 37, 38, 45, 48, 51, 55, 58/9, 60, 66, 75, 76, 81, 96, 116, 119, 125, 132/3, 137, 147, 161
John Melville: page 13(l)
Brian Nash: page 107
Peter Reilley: pages 24, 42, 85, 87, 90, 102, 129, 141, 144, 153, 157, 158, 162